MICHAEL J. BIRD

THE TOWN THAT DIED

A Chronicle of the Halifax Explosion

NIMBUS
PUBLISHING

To Olive,
as a small token of my gratitude

Nimbus Publishing Limited
3731 Mackintosh St, Halifax, NS B3K 5A5
(902) 455-4286 nimbus.ca

Printed and bound in Canada
Design: Jonathan Rotsztain

Library and Archives Canada Cataloguing in Publication

    Bird, Michael J., 1928-
    The town that died : a chronicle of the Halifax Explosion /
    Michael J. Bird.

    ISBN 978-1-55109-842-5

1. Halifax Explosion, Halifax, N.S., 1917. I. Title.

FC2346.4.B57 2011   971.6'22503   C2011-900036-9

Canada | The Canada Council Le Conseil des Arts for the Arts | du Canada | NOVA SCOTIA Communities, Culture and Heritage

Nimbus Publishing acknowledges the financial support for its publishing activities from the Government of Canada through the Canada Book Fund (CBF) and the Canada Council for the Arts, and from the Province of Nova Scotia through the Department of Communities, Culture and Heritage.

TABLE OF CONTENTS

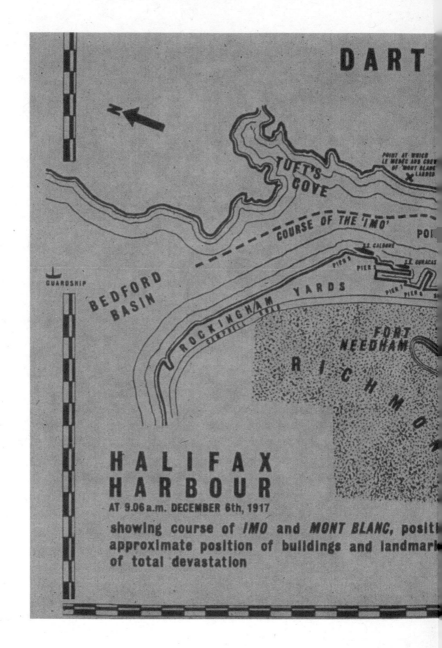

DART

POINT AT WHICH
LE MEDEC AND CREW
OF 'MONT BLANC'
LANDED

TUFT'S
COVE

COURSE OF THE 'IMO'

POI

GUARDSHIP

BEDFORD
BASIN

S.S. CALONNE

PIER 9

PIER

S.S. CURACAS

PIER 7

PIER 8

ROCKINGHAM YARDS

CAMPBELL ROAD

FORT
NEEDHAM

RICHMO

HALIFAX
HARBOUR

AT 9.06 a.m. DECEMBER 6th, 1917

showing course of *IMO* and *MONT BLANC*, positi
approximate position of buildings and landmark
of total devastation

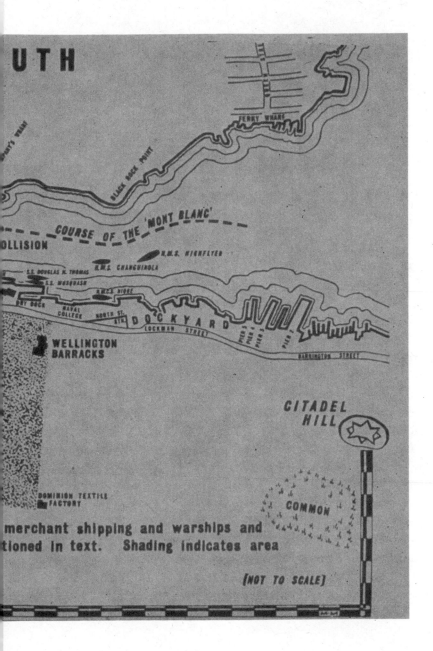

UTH

FERRY WHARE

GRANT'S WHARF

BLACK ROCK POINT

COURSE OF THE 'MONT BLANC'

OLLISION

H.M.S. HIGHFLYER

S.S. DOUGLAS H. THOMAS

H.M.S. CHANGUINOLA

S.S. MUSQUASH

H.M.C.S. NIOBE

DRY DOCK

NAVAL COLLEGE

NORTH ST.

D O C K Y A R D

LOCKMAN STREET

PIER 4 PIER 5 PIER 6

PIER 2

WELLINGTON BARRACKS

BARRINGTON STREET

CITADEL HILL

DOMINION TEXTILE FACTORY

COMMON

merchant shipping and warships and
tioned in text.   Shading indicates area

[NOT TO SCALE]

PROLOGUE

The *Acadian* was fifteen miles out of Halifax, Nova Scotia, and making good speed. The morning was brilliantly sunny, but cold, and from the bridge of the steamer Captain Campbell looked out toward the low-lying coastline and the city beyond.

Suddenly the scene was thrown into relief by a flash brighter than the sun. An immense cloud of smoke shot up into the air above Halifax crowned by an angry, crimson ball of rolling flames. Almost at once the flames were swallowed up in the black-grey smoke but from time to time they reappeared, boiling in its midst.

The billowing mass rolled higher and higher and then, after a few seconds, Campbell heard two thundering reports in quick succession.

The captain's sextant lay near at hand and, grabbing it, he took an observation of the summit of the smoke, now flattened and spreading outwards. His rapid calculations showed that it had risen to more than twelve thousand feet.

Fifteen minutes later the vast cloud was still visible. Now it hung, almost motionless, like an open umbrella over the funeral pyre of the town that died.

CHAPTER ONE
"WE ARE ALL EXPLOSIVES"

A little after one o'clock on Wednesday, December 5, 1917, Captain Aimé Le Medec entered the wheelhouse of the French freighter *Mont Blanc*. He had just worked out the ship's position as at one precisely and now he checked the compass before the helmsman. He nodded his satisfaction at the bearing to First Officer Jean Glotin and then went out onto the bridge.

The French ship had cleared New York at 11:00 P.M. on December 1 and from that moment Le Medec, fearfully conscious of the possibility of a marauding U-boat, had run as close inshore as he dared. From Newport to Bar Harbour the *Mont Blanc* had hugged the American coast. Off Bar Harbour, however, he had been forced to leave these comparatively safe waters and to head his vessel out into the open sea for a landfall at Yarmouth.

The one hundred mile crossing of the mouth of the Bay of Fundy had been tense but uneventful and now, away to port, the flat and rocky coast of Nova Scotia continued to offer further sanctuary.

The *Mont Blanc* was steaming at full speed some nine miles southwest of Pennant Point. In another hour or so she would round Cape Sambro and from there Le Medec would make for the examination anchorage between Lighthouse Bank and McNabs Island in accordance with the instructions given to him on sailing. Once in the anchorage, with formalities concluded and a pilot aboard, the *Mont Blanc* would proceed up-channel into Halifax Harbour.

Through the windows of the wheelhouse, Helmsman Marcel Aleton momentarily allowed his attention to wander. Idly he watched the captain as Le Medec slowly paced the bridge, deep in thought. "He is a worried man, our Commandant," Aleton was later to report to other members of the crew, "and who can blame him with such a cargo as ours in this bloody old hulk?"

Aleton's was a fair enough general description of the condition of the *Mont Blanc* for the small, 3,121-ton freighter had been badly used and hard worked during her sea time, but she was certainly not nearly as old as many another and prouder ship then in service.

Built by Sir Raylton Dixon & Company in their Middlesbrough shipyard, she had been launched in 1899 and purchased by E. Anquetil of Rouen who had held her for charter to all comers and for every type of cargo. Giddy with the profits to be made during the transportation boom of the early years of this century, Anquetil, who would concede only the most vital repairs and who had provided the minimum amount of maintenance, had pushed his ship to the very limits of safety and sea-worthiness.

It was then an already tired and neglected *Mont Blanc* that the reputable Compagnie Générale Transatlantique bought in 1915. It is doubtful whether at any other time they would have considered adding such a vessel to their well-known fleet but the urgent need for any and all ships to counter-balance the heavy toll levied by U-boats against the Allied merchant marine gave them no alternative. So it was that patched, painted, and overhauled as thoroughly as possible and with St. Nazaire as her new port of registry, and with a light gun mounted forward and another aft, the *Mont Blanc* went to war.

During the 1914–18 hostilities, all French merchant ships above a certain tonnage and of sizeable capacity came under the control of the French admiralty. This was achieved not by requisition of the vessels themselves, but indirectly by a government order mobilizing all merchant marine officers into the Naval Reserve. Therefore, whilst the *Mont Blanc* was, on paper, operated by her new owners, she came under navy orders as to the cargoes she carried and movement control, and almost immediately upon acquisition by the Compagnie Générale Transatlantique she was put into active service.

For many months, following the United States declaration of war on Germany on April 6, 1917, she sailed the Atlantic uneventfully, carrying on her outward journeys with general cargo for North America and returning to Europe laden with vital raw materials for the French war effort. When, however, on November 25, 1917, she berthed in Gravesend Bay, New York, there was a more sinister shipment awaiting her, and on this voyage the *Mont Blanc* had a new master.

Not more than five feet and four inches in height, but well built, with a neatly trimmed black beard to add authority to his somewhat youthful face, and with, as a Canadian newspaper man was later to report, "a broad forehead over snapping dark eyes," Captain Aimé Le Medec was thirty-eight years old when he assumed command and joined the ship at Bordeaux. To back his appointment he had more than twenty-two years' experience of the sea and he had seen over eleven years' service with the Compagnie Générale Transatlantique. On the summary of his service notes, kept in the records of their Paris office, it is constantly emphasized that he was "of a serious and modest character with remarkable qualities as an active and conscientious officer." A contemporary, however, describes him as a likeable but moody man at times inclined to be truculent, and as a competent, rather than a brilliant, sailor.

Nevertheless, Le Medec's steady promotion had followed the normal pattern of an officer in whom his employers had every confidence. From second officer when he joined the company at twenty-seven in 1906, he had risen through first officer to captain by 1916 when he was given the *Antilles*. The following year, but for a brief period only, he was master of the *Adb-el-Kader*.

Immediately upon his appointment to the *Mont Blanc* he had impressed upon her four officers his intention of working "strictly to the book," and had set about tightening discipline and improving efficiency among the thirty-six men of her mixed French and French Colonial crew.

At first resentful of his demands upon them, the men quickly came to respect and trust their captain, and Le Medec was reasonably happy with his new command when his ship tied up in Gravesend Bay. True, the misused *Mont Blanc* was no great prize to an ambitious young officer, but he accepted her as one further step up the ladder of his career, confident in his ability as a seaman, equal to any hazard of his profession in peace or war.

Never for one second, however, could he have imagined, on that November morning, the horror that was so soon to come.

The first intimation that Le Medec had of the nature of his new cargo was when he received instructions to allow on board a gang of shipwrights who were to construct special wooden linings for all four holds and erect partitions in each between-deck section. They worked throughout a day and a night nailing the planks carefully into position with copper nails. It was these nails that gave the captain his second clue, for he knew that copper is used when it is necessary to eliminate the possibility of sparks in the event of a sudden blow or shock.

French munitions ship *Mont Blanc* in Halifax harbour. The vessel had left New York and steamed its way to Halifax in order to join a war-time convoy going overseas.

When the shipwrights had finished there was not one steel plate or stanchion visible where they had been. Even the lining of the hold covers and the battening bars were sheathed in wood and Le Medec, with fluttering anxiety in the pit of his stomach, went ashore to have his suspicions confirmed.

"It's explosives, I'm afraid, on this trip," the French government agent told him. "A rather large shipment. You understand that normally we wouldn't use the *Mont Blanc* for this type of work, but we're short of ships so we have no choice."

Two days later the stevedores started to load. They worked slowly and carefully, and their feet were wrapped in linen cloths. Into the four holds went barrels and kegs of wet and dry picric acid, the deadly and sensitive lyddite that was the chief explosive agent of World War One, with a destructive power greater than that of TNT. Two of the 'tween-deck spaces were taken up exclusively with more picric acid, whilst the 'tween-deck furthest aft was stacked high with cases and kegs of trinitrotoluene. The lyddite in 'tween-deck No. 2 was so partitioned as to allow for more TNT to be stored in the starboard fore section. Between this TNT and the barrels of wet picric acid in No. 2 hold went cases of gun cotton.

When all had been secured and the hold covers, insulated with tarred cloth, had been gently closed and screwed tightly down so that the holds were hermetically sealed, even then the stevedores were not finished. The government agent had received last minute instructions from France to ship additional cargo that was urgently required. So onto the fore- and afterdecks were swung heavy metal drums, which were stacked three and four high and held in place with retaining boards and lashed with ropes. The liquid in these drums gave off the heady reek of benzole, the new super gasoline.

The manifest that was handed to her captain when the *Mont Blanc* was finally loaded, and the dock cranes had shunted away from her side, listed her complete cargo as 2,300 tons of picric acid, 200 tons of TNT, 35 tons of benzole, and 10 tons of gun cotton. Her destination: Bordeaux.

All the hideous ingredients were now assembled for the most disastrous explosion in the history of mankind prior to the atomic bomb and, out in the grey Atlantic, the trigger of this explosion, the Norwegian ship *Imo*, was making good speed on her voyage from Rotterdam to Halifax to keep her appointment with destiny.

If his cargo disturbed him, for he had never carried explosives before and his inexperience made him understandably nervous at the prospect of commanding a floating munitions dump, a greater shock awaited Le Medec when he was interviewed by the Senior British Naval Officer in New York.

He was told that the small convoy now assembling in the harbour would not accept him. The *Mont Blanc*'s three-cylinder, triple-expansion steam engine, which powered her single steel screw, was only capable, under normal conditions and when pushed to the maximum, of giving her a top speed of ten knots. Overloaded as she now was, it was doubtful whether she could even maintain seven-and-a-half knots for any great distance. The safety of every convoy depended largely upon a reasonable turn of speed, and a ship carrying munitions, and therefore stationed on the outer fringe, would need to make at least thirteen knots to keep up. The highly dangerous *Mont Blanc* would be too much of a lame duck for a group of vessels escorted by a single armed merchant cruiser.

His orders, therefore, were to proceed to Halifax, where it was just possible that his ship could be included in a larger convoy, sailing with many more escorts and with the added protection of a cruiser. It was, however, quite likely, the British Naval Officer added, that even under these conditions the *Mont Blanc*'s lack of speed would be considered too great a risk to any convoy, and in that event Le Medec would receive special orders in Halifax covering an independent Atlantic crossing.

Dusk was already closing in when the grey-painted *Mont Blanc*, low in the water to her winter plimsoll line and down by the head, and wallowing in a sea mildly excited by a freshening and chill breeze, came slowly into the examination anchorage under the scrutiny of a naval gunboat. On the bridge, Le Medec, with First Officer Glotin by his side, sang out an order to the helmsman in the wheelhouse.

"Port your helm."

Aleton repeated the order to the captain through the open window and swung the wheel to port. Slowly the *Mont Blanc* answered and began a starboard turn, for in 1917 steering orders were helm orders, based upon the movement of the helm on the earliest sailing vessels. Therefore, on "port your helm," the wheel went to port but the rudder turned to starboard, bringing the ship's head also to starboard. This system was later to be changed so that universally today ships are steered by wheel orders and in the same way as a car, the wheel to starboard or port sending both rudder and bows in the same direction.

"Amidships. Steady she goes. Dead slow."

On the captain's last order, Third Officer Joseph Leveque, standing by the engine telegraph, rang down for a reduction in speed so that the pilot boat now bobbing toward the ship could come alongside.

Pilot Francis Mackey, a short, thickset man of forty-five with powerful hands and strong features, but with eyes a trifle red-rimmed with tiredness, took the dangling rope ladder as an expert and pivoted himself onto the deck of the *Mont Blanc* to be greeted by Captain Le Medec.

Mackey was a pilot with twenty-four years' experience taking ships in and out of the Port of Halifax. In all that time he had been involved in no accident of any kind and he was justifiably proud of his record. He was proud, too, of his Scottish ancestry, and of hailing from a tightly knit Nova Scotian village community of men, women, and children bound together by close intermarriage, the fear of God, and a distrust of any outsider.

Like all the Halifax pilots, Mackey was hard-pressed. The port, which in 1913 counted itself lucky to handle two million tons of shipping, now, at the height of the war boom, found itself swamped with cargo traffic in excess of seventeen million tons.

Despite this enormous increase in work, the pilots, very much a closed society and jealous of their status, had resolutely resisted and successfully obstructed the halfhearted demands of the admiralty and the "prairie sailors" of the newly formed Royal Canadian Navy that the Pilotage Commission grant licenses to any experienced man available, thus easing the strain. The men of Halifax were determined to keep within their insular fraternity all the work and all its rewards. And the rewards were great. It was not unusual for a pilot to take home in one month, as his equal share of their pooled fees, the then staggering sum of $1,000. Subsequent events were to prove that these same men were capable of even greater obstinacy.

As Le Medec took the pilot's outstretched hand, a situation became obvious that in the weeks to come was to be made much of by opposing KCs. Mackey spoke no French, and whilst the Captain of the *Mont Blanc* had a little English, he was unhappy using it as he became easily embarrassed on the many occasions when he had trouble in expressing himself. He was relieved, therefore, to find at their first meeting that the pilot seemed to understand his hesitant words well enough, even though, for his part, he had difficulty in following Mackey, who tended to speak too quickly.

Mackey informed the captain that he considered it unlikely, owing to the lateness of the hour, that the *Mont Blanc* would be allowed to pass into the harbour that night, as the movement of merchant vessels through the gate of the boom defence was prohibited between dusk and dawn. This was almost immediately confirmed by a signal from the gunboat instructing the ship to drop anchor and prepare for boarding by an examining officer.

Le Medec gave the necessary orders, and then suggested that the pilot remain on board overnight and take the *Mont Blanc* up-channel as early as possible next morning. Mackey accepted this suggestion readily and the two men went to the captain's cabin.

"I regret I cannot offer you a drink. It is not possible," Le Medec said haltingly, in an attempt to explain that since the outbreak of war it was prohibited for any French vessel to carry alcohol. Mackey nodded that he understood and Steward Duvicq was summoned to bring coffee.

As they waited, the pilot enquired the nature of the ship's cargo and Le Medec, without going into details as to quantity, told him. Mackey appeared satisfied and unconcerned.

Examining officer Lieutenant Terence Freeman, RCNVR, boarded the *Mont Blanc* at 4:36 P.M. and was taken straight to the captain's cabin. He acknowledged the Halifax pilot, whom he knew by sight and, after being introduced to Le Medec, he asked to see the ship's papers and cargo manifest. These were handed to him together with the orders that had been issued in New York, and as the Lieutenant examined the documents closely, Le Medec volunteered, "We are all explosives!"

Freeman, who had already noted this fact and found himself surprised at the exceptionally large quantity listed, nodded but made no comment. After a little while he returned the sheaf of papers to the captain and instructed him to remain at anchor until morning.

"Unless you hear from me to the contrary, you may proceed up harbour on a signal from my ship, which will be given as soon as it is light enough for good navigation. Around 07:15 hours I should say."

Le Medec was then given a number that he was told he must hoist in flags before entering the harbour. The examination formalities concluded, the naval officer shook hands and left the ship.

At 5:30 P.M. Lieutenant Freeman signaled the arrival of the French vessel and details of her cargo to the chief examining officer, Commander Frederick Wyatt, RNR, on HMCS *Niobe*. His signal was acknowledged.

Later that evening Aimé Le Medec paused on the bridge of the *Mont Blanc* for a moment to listen to the night sounds of the sea and watch the beam from the McNabs lighthouse and the powerful searchlights of the harbour defences sweeping and probing the dark water. Then he went to his cabin to dine with Mackey.

When the meal was over the two men sat and talked. Mackey brought out cigars and offered one to the captain, who shook his head. As the pilot struck a match, Le Medec, mindful of the posters prominently displayed throughout the ship, took the opportunity to remark, "In here it is all right to smoke, but nowhere else. It is even prohibited to carry matches in your pocket when on deck. On this voyage, a fire or a big bump and the whole damned *Mont Blanc* is no more!"

As the small cabin clouded with cigar smoke, some six miles away, in the broad expanse of Bedford Basin, the normally jovial Captain Haakon From cursed again his ship's agents. They had known of his desire to clear Halifax that day, and he had told them himself that he was short of fuel for his voyage to New York to pick up another cargo of urgently needed relief supplies for war-torn Belgium.

"The coal tender will be with you by 3:00 P.M. at the latest," they had promised the Norwegian, and From had believed them and had taken on a pilot.

At three o'clock there had been no sign of the fuel; neither was there an hour later; and all the while, as his ship waited, the captain's chances of sailing had receded with the dwindling light.

It was 5:30 P.M. when the tender finally came alongside and discharged fifty tons of best steam coal, but by then it was dark and the harbour boom was closed.

From cursed again at the delay forced upon him by incompetence over which he had no control. His one consolation was that the pilot, William Hayes, was aboard and so would be on hand in the morning to take the *Imo* through the Narrows and out to the open sea.

CHAPTER TWO

COLLISION IN THE NARROWS

William Fowlie leant back in his chair, stretched, and yawned widely. Although around him the office of the Halifax & Bermuda Cable Company, high up in the Dennis Building on Granville Street, was still quietly active, the long hours of the night shift had been furiously busy, with an almost ceaseless flow of inward and outward messages demanding the full attention of the eighteen-year-old operator. For the moment though, the key before him was silent and still. Suddenly he felt very tired and realized how welcome was the prospect of breakfast and then bed.

He stretched again and looked up at the clock on the office wall; it was 7:10 A.M. Not long to go now.

Outside, a light frost and the early morning mist that had risen off the harbour grudgingly gave way to a winter sun rising in an almost cloudless sky. The air was crisp and sharp and carried a promise of snow. Slowly at first, but with gathering momentum, Halifax was stirring to meet the wartime routine of Thursday, December 6.

By now the sidewalks were clear of that earlier procession of men and women making for the city's shipyards and factories. For them, work had begun at seven o'clock; for others it was still an hour or more away. Now there were only a few people about, and the tram trundling along Barrington Street was half empty, but through the residential areas whistling newsboys cycled their rounds, leaving an expertly aimed wake of morning papers. Already bannered above many a cup of steaming coffee was the *Herald* headline of the day: GERMANS START NEW OFFENSIVE TO TAKE VENICE; or that of the *Chronicle*: BRITISH HAVE SITUATION IN CONTROL AT CAMBRAI.

In the select houses spaciously set back in the quiet streets of the south end of the city, sleepy-eyed maids were filling kettles for the morning tea, or going from room to room opening the heavy curtains that had been drawn across the windows the night before in dutiful compliance with the dim-out regulations.

Starched and rustling nurses moved through the long and antiseptic wards of the newly built hospital on Camp Hill where, in neatly ordered and freshly made beds, lay the repatriated wounded from the Western Front. The patients talked and joked quietly amongst themselves, whilst here and there one would secretly drag on a cigarette held in a cupped hand beneath the covers and out of sight of a hawk-eyed sister.

From the side door of a shop off Water Street, a merchant seaman stepped out onto the dirt sidewalk. He gave a curt nod to the prostitute who had let him out, hawked loudly, spat into the roadway, and then rolled away in the direction of the waterfront. The girl stood watching him for a moment, taking in deep breaths of the morning air, and then the steady tread of a patrol returning to the dockyard or to Wellington Barracks sent her scuttling back inside and the door closed quietly behind her.

At the north end of town, and in a cloak of steam, a loaded freight train crawled over points and into the Canadian

Government Railway's marshalling yard. On one side of the railway tracks lay the upper piers of the harbour and on the other the district known as Richmond. Here, row upon row of shabby wooden houses crowded the streets that ran upward at a sharp incline from Campbell Road.

Richmond had none of the wealth and dignity of Young Avenue or the avenues on the Northwest Arm, where many of the town's leading citizens lived, nor even the middleclass comfort of Chebucto. For the most part it consisted of graceless working-class homes, over which now drifted a haze of grey smoke from the hundreds of hall stoves kept burning day and night against the winter cold.

Southward, Campbell Road became Lockman and then Barrington Street, a busy thoroughfare bisecting the city's business and commercial quarter, which was built on the steep slope of a hill crowned by the old Citadel fortress and skirted by the busy wharves of the harbour.

This splendid and well equipped waterfront not only provided Halifax with her *raison d'etre*, but also with the easiest approach to her sister town of Dartmouth. The first ferry of the morning had cast off crowded with workers for the various industries that the war had seen established in this small but rapidly expanding community a mile or so away on the opposite shore of the harbour. Now one of the little steamers, on a return journey, nudged the jetty at the foot of George Street.

To the north of Richmond and the CGR freight yard was Rockhead Prison and the slum of tarpaper houses called Africville. This mean suburb straggled along one shore of Bedford Basin where, across the water, the crew of the *Imo* were now busily preparing their ship for sailing.

The *Mont Blanc*'s third officer wiped the lens of his binoculars with a handkerchief and then leaned forward over the bridge with the glasses in his hand. Leveque had come on duty at seven o'clock, and for the past twenty minutes he had been watching the Canadian gunboat and waiting for her signal to the ship to enter the harbour. An American freighter lying some way to starboard had already received clearance and was now getting under way, her propeller beating the sea at her stern into foam. With a full head of steam and the watch primed to weigh anchor, the *Mont Blanc* was ready to follow.

A few minutes before 7:30, Captain Le Medec, accompanied by Pilot Mackey, joined the third officer on the bridge. Almost upon their arrival, a signal lamp began to blink from the gunboat and Mackey read off the message.

"*Mont Blanc.* Hoist identification. Proceed Bedford Basin to await further orders."

With a grunt of satisfaction, Le Medec sang down the command to get the anchor in to First Officer Glotin who, in turn, relayed it to the bo'sun on the forecastle. Then the captain turned to Leveque and handed him a slip of paper on which was written the code number that Lieutenant Freeman had given him the night before.

"Have this run up," he ordered.

Leveque took the paper and moved to obey. Then he stopped, turned in his tracks, and asked, "The red flag for explosives also, sir?"

The question seemed to take Le Medec almost by surprise. For a moment he stared thoughtfully at the young officer and then he shook his head. "No, it is not necessary."

Seaman Alphonse Serre was already at the helm, and when the flags had been hoisted Leveque took up his station by the engine room telegraph. The first officer reported that the anchor was secured, and Le Medec, his hands thrust deeply into the pockets of his greatcoat, nodded to the pilot to take over.

"Half speed ahead."

"*En avant à demi-vitesse*," interpreted the captain.

The telegraph jangled and, vibrating under the steadily increasing beat of her engine, the *Mont Blanc* moved out into the main stream of the harbour approach.

Over in Dartmouth, at 48 Queen Street, a narrow street of wooden houses that ran down almost to the shore, Bessie Fraser was between breakfasts. Her husband, Alexander, had eaten his earlier before leaving for work in the Dartmouth shipyards, but soon the children would be clamouring for theirs. Already Mrs. Fraser could hear the pad of feet on the floor of the room above and muted squeals as four-year-old William romped with his younger sister, Hattie. Before long, the noise would wake the baby in his cot and then the day would really have begun.

Bessie placed a saucepan of porridge over a low flame on the gas cooker and remembered as she did so that she still had to light the kitchen stove, and that, before she could, kindling would have to be chopped. A heavy thump and a cry of fury from upstairs halted her at the head of the steps leading to the basement fuel store. The stove could wait, she decided, and instead she went up to restore peace and dress the children.

Pilot William Hayes was keenly aware that the silent Captain From standing beside him on the bridge was still very upset over the delay in sailing and, in his opinion, the Norwegian had good cause. Had the agents not bungled the loading of the coal, the *Imo*, protected from U-boat attack by the words BELGIAN RELIEF painted in huge red letters against a white background on her either side, could have by now, on a direct course and at a steady speed of twelve to thirteen knots, been well out to sea and almost halfway to New York.

When at 8:10 A.M. the relief ship finally got under way, the sympathetic pilot was determined that, for his part, he would do what he could to see that she lost no further time and, once he had slowly zigzagged through the other vessels anchored in the Basin, he rang down for more speed. As a result, the *Imo* was making close on seven knots and her speed was still increasing when she entered the Narrows, the mile long and five-hundred-yard wide channel connecting Bedford Basin with the waters of Halifax Harbour proper.

It was at this moment that Hayes first saw the inward bound American freighter steadily approaching him.

Standing on the corner of Kempt Road and Robie Street, the Dominion Textile Company's ugly, greystone cotton factory was alive with the hum of wartime boom business.

At one of the spinning machines amid the noisy clatter of the third floor, nineteen-year-old Lillian Atkins watched with a practised eye as the combed cotton fibre "rovings" before her were drawn and twisted into strong threads.

Lillian had only been with Dominion a few weeks but, quick to learn, she had soon picked the job up and now felt as much at ease with the work as if she had been doing it for years.

Like so many others, she had been drawn to Halifax from a small Nova Scotian town, in her case Yarmouth on the southwestern shore of the province, by letters from friends that told of the plentiful work and of the excitement of life in a big garrison and dockyard city. An orphan, there had been little to hold her in her hometown, and on the whole she was happy that she had made the change. She had secured a job with the textile company before she left Yarmouth, and so a representative of the firm had met her at the station and taken her to a boarding house, where she was now treated more as a daughter than as a mere lodger. True, the factory hours were long and the pay not quite so munificent as it had first sounded when weighed against big city prices, but Lillian was content.

As she worked, her mind was only half on the spinning. Her other thoughts were for the evening ahead. What to do? That was the problem. There was a war film showing at one of the cinemas, *The Rape of Belgium*. But no, a friend who had seen it had reported that it had made her cry. Still, it should be exciting, and a good cry never hurt anyone did it? Then again, a soda and a gossip downtown with some of the other girls might be fun.

It was now 8:21 A.M.

The sea between McNabs Island and Point Pleasant was sown with a protective screen of mines, and the only safe passage was through a strip of water covered by the searchlight and artillery batteries on either shore. At a crawl of four knots, the limit in the port set by the admiralty being five knots, the *Mont Blanc*, under Mackey's guidance, approached the harbour boom which, together with an anti-submarine net of heavy steel cable, ran from the New Terminal's breakwater to Ives Point. Already the signal was up that indicated that the passage was open for the French ship, and slowly she slid between the red-painted gate vessel and the gently rolling hinge buoy.

Mackey was well aware that Article 25 of the *Regulations for Preventing Collisions at Sea* stipulated that, "In narrow channels every steam vessel shall, when it is safe and practicable, keep to that side of the fairway or mid-channel which lies on the starboard side of such vessel." Accordingly, he took the *Mont Blanc* up-channel well over toward the Dartmouth shore, and fifteen minutes after clearing the boom she passed through the eastern gate of the harbour's inner line of net defences, which were strung out from George's Island.

To the pilot this was just another routine job. Apart from a slight haze to westward, visibility was excellent, enabling him to shape his course solely from the landmarks he knew so well. From now on it would be plain sailing right through into Bedford Basin.

The messroom of the Royal Naval College was unusually quiet. Normally breakfast, like every other meal, was taken in an atmosphere of excited chatter, but today an air of almost impending doom seemed to have dampened even the most boisterous spirit.

Uppermost in the thoughts of the junior cadets was the dread ordeal of the end-of-term examinations, which were due to begin later in the morning. The seniors were even more concerned about their final exam, which was now only two days away.

Cadet "Billy" Brock was not, however, unduly depressed. He had enjoyed his first term at the college and had quickly come to terms with the discipline and rigid routine that the navy imposed upon its fifteen-year-old future officers. His marks in the previous tests had been steady, and he now faced the prospect of the examination with reasonable confidence.

The Royal Naval College of Canada was, like the Canadian Navy, very much in its infancy and something of an experiment. Run on the lines of its English example, Dartmouth, by Commander E. A. E. Nixon, RN, now transferred to the RCN, it catered for only a limited number of cadets. Its present establishment was four seniors, fourteen intermediates, and twenty juniors such as Brock.

The college was housed at the north end of the Halifax dockyard in a severe red brick building that had once served as a naval hospital. The pair of brass cannons that flanked the steps of the main entrance were pointed out over a narrow pathway beyond, which a lawn swept away to the dockyard wall. To the rear of the building, on the far side of a terrace, lay a tennis court, a collection of wooden huts, and the southern extreme of the Narrows.

Imo on the Dartmouth shore after the explosion. The Norwegian relief vessel was a neutral ship en route from Europe to New York to pick up relief supplies for Belgium.

Brock finished his meal and got up from the table. There was still some time to go until the first warning gong for "divisions" was sounded; time that could be usefully employed in cramming. On the way out of the messroom he passed by Kenneth Mackenzie, his Cadet Captain and one of the seniors due to graduate that term. The older boy was lost in thought.

Lieutenant Richard Woollams, RNR, officer of the watch on board HMS *Highflyer*, was pacing the starboard side of the quarterdeck when the *Mont Blanc* passed at a distance of about a hundred yards.

Highflyer was a 5,600-ton protected cruiser of the Hermes class. She had arrived in Halifax on December 1, and now lay anchored in mid-channel, her port side at an angle of about 120° to the Halifax shore.

Earlier in the war, the cruiser had distinguished herself when, in action against commerce raiders, she had engaged and sunk the much larger auxiliary cruiser *Kaiser Wilhelm der Grosse* at the moment when the German ship was in the act of taking the British steamer *Galician* as a prize off Rio del Oro. Under the command of Captain H. N. Garnett, RN, she was at present engaged in Atlantic convoy escort duty.

The officer of the watch cast an interested and critical eye over the heavily laden steamer and the metal drums stacked on her decks. "Fuel oil, or perhaps petrol," he mused. "Whatever it is, she's damned sloppily loaded. No speed either. The convoy admiral won't be very happy about that one!" As he watched, the *Mont Blanc* dipped her colours in salute.

From the bridge, Le Medec saw the *Highflyer's* ensign lowered in acknowledgement, and then the cruiser slowly fell away astern. A minute or so later, Mackey sighted the *Imo* for the first time as she took the bend where the Narrows turned westward into Bedford Basin. She was still about three-quarters of a mile away, but steaming at speed and, to his surprise, heading southeast quarter south. A course which, if continued, would intercept that of the *Mont Blanc*.

"Looks as though that damned fool ahead is aiming to come down in our water," he muttered to Le Medec, and then burst out angrily, "Why the devil doesn't he get over to his own side? Better give him a whistle." The captain nodded and, reaching for the cord that hung between the windows of the wheelhouse, he tugged at it sharply.

The ship's whistle gave one short blast, a signal that would normally indicate the *Mont Blanc* was altering course to starboard, but which in this case was primarily intended to establish her claim to that side of the channel. But even before the rasping note faded on the morning air, Mackey had decided that, merely as a precaution, it might be advisable to follow through and take the ship a little over to the right and reduce speed to the minimum.

"Port your helm. Dead slow."

Leveque put the engine telegraph handle hard over, first to the *Attention* position and then to *Lentement*, as the pilot's orders were translated and the helmsman spun the wheel to bring the *Mont Blanc* to within three hundred feet of the Dartmouth shore.

Mackey was convinced that the trespasser would now give way, swing over to mid-channel, and so pass port to port as the regulations stipulated. He was, therefore, thunderstruck when, seconds later, the *Imo* replied with two short blasts meaning, "I am altering my course to port." This would put the outward bound and much larger ship even further into his water and across his bows.

"What the hell?" he roared, and then quickly ordered, "Hard aport. Stop engines." At the same time he gestured to the captain to repeat the one blast signal.

By now the *Imo* was drawing dangerously close, and Mackey and Le Medec felt a chill of fear as she again answered the *Mont Blanc* with two blasts and held her course.

"They're getting kinda nervous out there," observed the chief engineer of the *Douglas H. Thomas* as, across the channel, whistle signal followed whistle signal in quick succession.

He was leaning over the deck rail with the captain of the tug that was tied up alongside one of the steamers moored against the Halifax dry dock wharf, and both men were interested spectators of the confusion off the opposite shore.

The captain nodded thoughtfully and took another swig of tea from the white mug clenched in his fist. The two ships were certainly asking for trouble, especially the Norwegian, but surely, with visibility so good and plenty of open water, there could be no real risk to either. Unless, of course, someone did something really foolish.

With beads of sweat breaking out on his forehead, Mackey realized that there was now only one course open to him if he was to avert a collision, and that was to go to port and permit the *Imo* to pass starboard to starboard. Snatching at the whistle cord, he blew two blasts to warn the other vessel of his intentions. Simultaneously, the captain, who had also decided that this was the only possible maneuver for his vessel, shouted to Serre in the wheelhouse.

"Bear all to the left."

Although the engine of the *Mont Blanc* had stopped, the overloaded ship still maintained some little speed, and so answered to her helm when it was put hard astarboard.

Sluggishly the French freighter turned away from the Dartmouth shore, and for a moment the two vessels were brought onto opposite and parallel courses. But, almost as the *Mont Blanc* turned, the *Imo* sounded three short blasts signalling that she was putting her engines full speed astern. As she did so, Captain Le Medec saw to his horror that this action was veering her head to starboard and that, with her forward motion not yet checked by her reversed propeller, a collision was now inevitable.

Seconds later, the bow of the *Imo* struck the *Mont Blanc* and, in a shower of sparks, ripped through the plating of her No. 1 hold.

Seven-year-old Edith O'Connell turned from a window of her home on Campbell Road, through which she had been gazing out over the waters of the Narrows opposite in company with her younger sister, Lulu, and exclaimed excitedly, "Two ships have just bumped out here, and now one of them is on fire."

CHAPTER THREE

THE DAYS BEFORE

In June 1749, the Honourable Edward Cornwallis in the sloop *Sphinx* sailed into a broad anchorage on the east coast of Canada that the local *Meeg-a-maage* tribe called *Che-book-took*. Cornwallis brought with him in thirteen transports: 2,576 "settlers" comprised for the most part of the gutter sweepings of London.

This colonizing rabble quickly anglicized the name of their haven to Chebucto, re-christened the natives "Micmacs," embarked upon the systematic slaughter of all those members of the tribe whom they could not exploit, and built a fortified settlement which they named after the noble lord, President of the Board of Trade and Plantations, who had dispatched them there.

Thus Halifax was born.

Whilst by 1900, Halifax, capital of the province of Nova Scotia and incorporated as a city in 1841, had expanded beyond even Cornwallis's wildest dreams, the Atlantic seaport had never attempted, nor shown any desire, to keep pace with the vital and bustling development evident in other communities throughout the Dominion. To many Canadians at that time, the name of

Halifax was synonymous with smug self-satisfaction and the very worst aspects of conservatism. And not without reason.

An historic city, she gloried in the past and, looking backward too much and too long, had been content to let the challenge presented to a young nation to forge a new and individual way of life go unheeded while she remained an aloof and almost alien spectator.

For more than 150 years the Imperial army and navy had been the life-blood of the town, and in return Halifax had served the Empire well both as a garrison city and a dockyard. For its part of the bargain, Whitehall had kept and cosseted her and, by providing steady employment and profit for the majority of her people, had protected her from the need to venture far into the world of competitive commerce and industry, with all its uncertainties and winds of change. Accordingly, the Haligonians of 1900, although steadfastly refusing to admit it even to themselves, were the lethargic and anemic citizens of a stagnant backwater.

For a few years following the turn of the century, life in the city followed its unruffled and traditional pattern. Class divisions were clear-cut and instituted by the Almighty for the benefit of society in general. To all men, a prerequisite of happiness was to recognize their station in life and to accept it without question. The poor were the poor and the rich were the rich, and the latter, at least, had every intention of preserving the status quo.

The sidewalks were thick with British soldiers and sailors, and the money rolled in. The members of the Nova Scotia Legislature that met in the provincial Parliament Building each February were not overburdened with responsibility, and even if the heart of the city was sandwiched between two offensive, vice-ridden slums, and had been since its earliest days, this was of little concern to the Haligonian social set as it sallied forth to attend yet another ball or garden party given by the Lieutenant Governor at Government House.

On summer afternoons, excursion steamers took visitors for a trip around the harbour, where much of the might of the North American Squadron lay at anchor. At the select Halifax golf course, playing members teed off against visiting naval officers who, by way of returning the hospitality, would often bring with them the ship's band to divert the ladies as, under gay umbrellas, they sipped their tea and gossiped.

There were concerts, too, in the Public Gardens, open to all, and in the evening, dancing on the lawns under Chinese lanterns. For naval and army officers and the gentlemen of the city there was the ritual of cricket and cucumber sandwiches on the Garrison Grounds. For the working classes there was baseball on the Common.

Everything was ordered and nothing changed. Britannia ruled the waves and paid the bills. God was in His Heaven and all was well with the world. Then, all at once, the spell was broken.

Events were moving rapidly in Europe. The threat of German ambitions loomed large, and England set about recalling her armed forces to be ready for the clash that, sooner or later, was bound to come. Whilst the admiralty drastically reduced the North American Squadron to little more than a token force and transferred its headquarters to Bermuda, the army began the steady withdrawal of the garrison. The life-blood of Halifax was all too quickly draining away.

By February 1906, the withdrawal was complete and the soldiers and sailors were gone, leaving behind them, as a legacy to the Canadian Department of Militia and Defence, tons of equipment, empty and echoing barracks, windswept parade grounds, and a lifeless dockyard. The city was on her own for the first time in her history and, ill-prepared for the day and with the props of Whitehall support kicked from under her, fell into an economic decline.

Three things saved Halifax from becoming a town of total despair. Firstly, the imagination and drive of a few go-ahead men, previously frustrated by snobbery and the traditionalist attitude, who seized upon the moment to introduce more industry into the city. In time, new factories sprang up whilst existing ones were enlarged, and the city slowly set about meeting its responsibilities as the business and commercial centre of Nova Scotia; a responsibility that hitherto it had sadly neglected.

Secondly, the Canadian government, after years of indifference, and as if suddenly realizing the importance of the Atlantic seaport as something other than a mere transit point for the immigrant multitude heading for the West, embarked upon imaginative and costly plans for the development of the harbour and port facilities.

This development was still not completed when an event occurred that was to prove the third and most important contributory factor in the salvation of Halifax. On August 4, 1914, England declared war on Germany.

When the British forces withdrew in 1906, Canada was left with only an insignificant army and no naval forces whatever with which to protect herself. The Dominion government, with other and seemingly more important matters on hand, viewed this new responsibility for defence with disinterest and responded to it with nothing more than a gesture. The Royal Canadian Regiment and a small force of artillery, which together constituted almost the nation's entire military strength, were quartered in Wellington Barracks, ostensibly to guard Halifax, and then forgotten.

Despite pressure from many quarters, nothing positive was done about setting up a navy until 1911, when the new federal Conservative government headed by Sir Robert Borden took office. Even then, the bitter attacks and parliamentary tactics of the Liberal opposition cut Borden's plans almost to ribbons, with the result that when, at last, Canada was able to boast of an Atlantic fleet of her own it consisted solely of the cruiser *Niobe*, purchased from Britain and already out of date.

The cruiser arrived to fanfares and jubilation, and then, within twelve months, was berthed at the Halifax dockyard and left coal-less and forlorn. Meanwhile, with great enthusiasm, the newly established Royal Canadian Naval College set about training officers for a navy that in reality did not exist.

This position was relatively unchanged when Canada entered the war alongside the mother country so that, whilst the Dominion was able to contribute to the struggle an army hastily strengthened by eager volunteers, it was left to the Royal Navy alone to keep open the Atlantic sea lanes, using as its North American base the city it had deserted eight years earlier.

Many of the British sailors who returned to Halifax in 1914 had seen peacetime service in the dockyard and, although the city was going through a minor revolution, outwardly she appeared to them to have changed but little.

The old wooden houses that on every hand bordered the shelving streets remained unpainted and neglected. The town was still cursed with an antiquated garbage system and offensive gutters. It had the best water in Nova Scotia but the poorest water system ever inspected, and an obsolete tramway network with its tracks laid out through unpaved streets that were knee-deep in mud in autumn, and furious rivers of choking dust in the summer winds.

There were few automobiles, and the traffic was made up for the most part of Halifax "slovens," low-slung drays with a high-perched driver's seat that were invariably drawn by a pair of Clydesdales, and the lighter, all-purpose "teams," the boxed-in delivery wagons so popular with tradesmen. Despite their name, these teams were pulled by a single horse and for use over the winter snow could be fitted with sledge-runners instead of wheels.

It was still not uncommon to see an ox cart in the main thoroughfares, and only the business section and a few of the upper-class residential streets had concrete sidewalks. Everywhere else, pedestrians walked on pavements of household cinders.

Throughout the city there was a melancholy air of civic backwardness, which belied the sensational boom that the European conflict had brought to Halifax, and which steadily increased with every passing year. For with the war came not only the Royal Navy to be victualled, serviced, fuelled, and entertained, but the thousands of allied cargo ships that put into the harbour to await convoy to Europe, bringing with them crews with money to burn and supply needs to be filled.

From all sides, merchants found themselves presented with orders for eggs by the thousand dozen, and equivalent quantities of meat and other provisions. In an hour, an unscrupulous trader with only a small business could make upwards of £500 in pound notes by selling tinned butter and ham at exorbitant sums to sailors returning to rationed Europe.

The factories of Halifax and Dartmouth worked at fever pitch to produce sugar, textiles, iron and steel, and other manufactured goods now vitally important and fetching premium prices. While ships in need of repair queued for a place in the bustling shipyards, export figures shot up from $19,157,170 in 1915 to $142,000,000 in 1917, and bank clearings totalled $152,000,000 in this same year.

The Haligonians were reaping a golden harvest, and from all over the country people poured into the city determined to get their share. The last pre-war census of 1911 had recorded a population of 46,619 and had predicted an annual increase of between 3 and 5 percent, but the surge of newcomers quickly made nonsense of these figures. Rents and prices soared, but still they came. They came to work, to buy, to sell, and some came to steal and exploit, but all had the same purpose in mind—to make big money.

The principal source of undercover revenue was prostitution, and each day saw the arrival of scores of streetwalkers and trollops, of every refinement and from all over Canada, eager to supplement the services provided by the established and harassed local corps. Brothels blossomed through the old quarter and along Water Street like buds in spring, and were eventually to be found even in hitherto respectable residential neighbourhoods.

The superior bordellos, catering to army and naval officers and the "carriage-trade," operated discreetly from well-appointed and exotically furnished houses. The "short-time" girls plied their trade in less luxurious surroundings, often in the back room of a small shop that outwardly sold cigarettes and tobacco, and which provided nothing more elaborate than a bed in one of three or four cubicles and a bowl of disinfectant.

Periodically the police made raids on the more clearly defined red-light districts and, if not tipped off in advance by someone on the force with an itching palm and a growing bank-balance, some of the girls would be arrested and hauled into court. These raids had little effect however; the prostitutes merely paid their fines, went away happily, and opened up a new establishment in some other part of town, and from then on it was business as usual.

Almost as numerous as the brothels were the speakeasies or "blind pigs," brought into being by an ill-conceived provincial law prohibiting the sale of intoxicating liquor, which came into effect on Dominion Day 1916. Catering to thousands of thirsty servicemen and merchant seamen, the wealthy owners of these back alley bars, dispensing wood alcohol gin and home-distilled whisky at prohibition prices, were, together with the few zealous reformers who had agitated for it, the only members of the community who did not doubt the wisdom of this Act.

So the boom was reflected throughout every activity of the city, and nowhere did it have a greater or more prosperous effect than upon the harbour, with its tremendous increase in tonnage handled. But here there was discontent.

Within weeks of the outbreak of war the entire administration of the port had been handed over to the admiralty, and whilst civilian harbour officials retained their positions, their responsibilities were greatly curtailed. They functioned largely as advisers whose advice, they felt, was more often than not disregarded. The majority resented the intrusion of naval officers into departments, which they considered could be more efficiently run on the old peacetime lines and by men with a greater knowledge of local conditions. They had little time, too, for the endless red tape of service procedure.

Whilst never openly airing their grievances, a number of them took to giving the minimum amount of co-operation in the hope that, through the resulting errors and minor delays, they would see their position vindicated.

If most of the harbour officials and, to an even greater extent, the pilots of Halifax resented the interference of British officers, they at least respected them as experienced men of the sea, and they greatly admired the glorious record and traditions of the Royal Navy. They felt very differently, however, about the officers of the young and struggling RCN who filled a number of vital posts in the naval command. Because the majority of these officers came from the vast interior rather than from the Maritime provinces, where the preference seemed strangely to be for service in the army, they were dismissed contemptuously as "prairie sailors" and upstart "freshwater admirals."

The Dominion as a whole seemed almost as devoid of naval sense as the United States, and the Canadian people had little confidence in or support for their new navy. Nowhere was this attitude more apparent than in the harbour of Halifax.

Any murmurs of discontent along the waterfront were, however, swallowed up and lost in the roaring pulse of the thriving community. It seemed as though the city had everything to look forward to and nothing to fear. The battlefields of the world with all their horror were a long way away, and surely there could be no danger to Halifax. True, there was talk of the possibility of Zeppelin raids or German bombardment from the sea, but the people refused to take either danger seriously and, whilst the anxious relatives of men away on active service prayed for peace and a happy reunion, the haunting fear of more than one complacent Haligonian was that the war might well end too soon and with it the bonanza.

At 8:45 A.M. on the morning of Thursday, December 6, 1917, the telephone rang in the house of the captain superintendent of the dockyard, and it was answered by Canadian Senior Naval Officer, Captain Frederick Claude Pasco, RCN, acting in the absence of the permanent captain superintendent, Captain Martin.

The call was from his office, to inform him that two merchant ships had collided in the Narrows and one of them was now on fire. In temporary command of the dockyard and all its resources, Pasco acted immediately. He cleared the line and then got through to the operator.

"Connect me with the transport officer, quickly."

The telephone went dead for a while and then the operator came on with, "I'm sorry, sir, but there is no answer from that office."

Pasco glanced at his watch and then ordered, "Try his home number." Thirty seconds ticked by before the operator cut in again. "That line is busy, sir."

The captain cursed softly and hung up. And then, swinging round on Martin's servant who had entered to clear the breakfast table, he said, "Get on this telephone and try and raise the transport officer. I can't wait any longer. There's a ship on fire in the harbour and I must see just what's going on out there."

The servant took the telephone and at the same time suggested, "Why not try your bedroom window, sir? You should get a pretty good view and that way you can use the extension up there when I get through."

Pasco nodded and ran upstairs. From his window he could see out beyond the dockyard to where a ship lay damaged but apparently motionless across the harbour. Billowing black smoke and a rolling ball of fire rose high into the air, but the vessel that was burning was hidden from sight behind some dockside buildings.

"It's a bad one all right," he muttered to himself. "Oil, probably."

He was craning his neck to get a better view when he heard the servant talking on the telephone from the room below, and he snatched up the extension by his bed. It was the transport office, but the transport officer had not yet arrived and Pasco was connected with Lieutenant Poole, the second-in-command.

"Captain Superintendent here, Poole. There's a merchantman on fire off Pier 6. Send the *Lee*, the *Gopher*, the *Musquash*, and any other tugs you have available with pumps, and get them there quickly. No, I don't know what she's carrying, looks like oil, but whatever it is, it's burning like hell!"

CHAPTER FOUR
"ABANDON SHIP"

From the bridge of the *Mont Blanc*, Le Medec and the pilot watched aghast and helpless as the *Imo's* bow cut, almost noiselessly, through the starboard side of the French ship to a depth of nine or ten feet. To their horror, they saw that, with the shock of the impact, some of the metal drums stacked forward were torn from their lashings and hurled in every direction, and that many of these burst open to cascade benzole over the deck and down through the open wound onto the lyddite in No. 1 'tween-deck.

Within seconds of the collision, the reversed propeller of the Norwegian vessel became effective so that her bow was now pulled back out of the jagged gash it had made in the plating of the *Mont Blanc*. Metal rasped against metal, and the friction threw out a rain of sparks, which instantly ignited the benzole that had seeped through into the hold. Thick black smoke began to pour from below deck, and by the time the *Imo* had drawn away a few yards to wallow helplessly with engines now stopped and steerage lost, the foredeck of the *Mont Blanc* was a sheet of flame.

As young Leveque and the helmsman, anxious but calm, waited for orders, Mackey seized the captain's arm urgently.

Although, as pilot, he was responsible for the ship whilst in the harbour, he felt in an emergency such as this only the master could finally decide what must be done, and it was obvious that Le Medec must act quickly.

The Frenchman did not move, but stood as if mesmerized by the fire below him, eyes wide and staring in a face drained of colour, his hands firmly gripping the grab-rail of the bridge. High on his right cheek a muscle twitched excitedly. Despite the cold morning air he could feel the sweat running down his body, and he fought to control the trembling in his legs.

His one thought was of the boxes and barrels of high explosives stacked in the hold. With the flames increasing and spreading, only God could know how long it would be before his hideous cargo was detonated. Le Medec was fearfully aware that his crew and thousands of people along the waterfront and in the town were in terrible danger, but what could he do? Desperately he searched for an answer. It was impossible even to attempt to put out the fire; there were no portable extinguishers on board, and if there had been, they would have been useless against such a blaze; and the only pressure hose connection on the *Mont Blanc* was on the forward deck, and anyone who tried to get to it now would certainly be burned to death.

The roaring inferno also ruled out any possibility of his men reaching and dropping the bow anchors to check the landward drift of the stricken vessel. The only other alternative, to open the seacock and scuttle the ship, would mean, before the water could flood in, at least half an hour's work on the rusted rivets and bolts securing the old-fashioned valve, and even then it would take another fifteen minutes or more for the freighter to sink.

Jean Glotin raced up onto the bridge for instructions. This was not his first experience of fire at sea. He was serving as second officer on the *Montreal* when, earlier in the war, she had been torpedoed and sunk in the Gulf of Gascony. He had seen panic then, and he saw it beginning to spread now through the crew of the *Mont Blanc*.

By this time, a pall of oily, black smoke rose two hundred or three hundred feet above the ship and the rolling flames, now bright orange, now blue, were level with the top of the foremast. As more of the intact metal drums exploded in the heat, scattering red-hot metal across the deck and adding to the blaze, there was little discipline left among the men milling in confusion around the lifeboats. It was the sound of terror in their voices as they shouted to one another that decided Le Medec. His first duty was clearly to his officers and crew. He swung round to give his orders and, as he did so, the pilot, more as a suggestion than any sort of command, said "Full speed ahead?"

As Mackey saw it, there was only one course open that might prevent an explosion, and that was to take the ship ahead at speed in an attempt to force enough sea water through the hole made by the *Imo* to extinguish the fire in No. 1 hold, whilst the crew fought the flaming benzole on deck. He did not know when he spoke that even if the first part of his plan were successful there was no equipment on board with which the second could be accomplished.

If Le Medec even heard the pilot, he gave no sign of having done so as he shouted to Glotin above the noise of the fire, "Abandon ship!"

The first officer sang out to the crew to get the lifeboats over the side, and Le Medec instructed Alphonse Serre to put the helm amidships and then go down with Leveque to boat stations.

There were two lifeboats on the *Mont Blanc*, both amidships, one on the port and one on the starboard side, and such was the frenzy of fear which had seized every member of the crew as they saw the fire gaining strength, that both had been swung outboard on their davits before any order had been given and one had even been lowered into the water. When the command to abandon ship came from the bridge, the second boat was let go and there was a wild rush for ladders and ropes. A witness to the scene was later to exclaim in court, "I have never seen two boats filled so quick in all my life."

By the time the captain, the pilot, and Glotin reached the deck, however, the mad scramble for places was over, oars were unshipped, and the crews were ready to pull away. Mackey lowered himself into the starboard lifeboat and, preceded by Glotin, the captain was halfway down the ladder on the port side when someone called out that Antoine Legat, the chief engineer, had not been seen on deck and that he was probably still in the engine room. Le Medec climbed back on board and went below.

The engine room was dark and hot, and heavy with the smell of oil. There was a gentle hiss of steam from somewhere around the motionless pistons, but there was no sign of anyone. Alone for the first time, a sudden feeling of despair and weariness swept over the captain that was so strong, he sank down onto an upturned crate and buried his face in his hands. A light touch on his shoulder made him look up again. It was Glotin.

"Captain, we must go. Legat is accounted for. When the others went up he remained to lift the safety valves on the boilers, but he is there now."

"You go, my friend. I am responsible and I must stay with the ship. It is correct, isn't it?"

"No, we will both go. Come, I don't think we have much time."

The first officer took Le Medec by the arm and gently pulled him to his feet. He made as if to protest again but, seeing it was useless, he smiled faintly, shrugged off the other's hand, and then followed him up on deck.

As soon as the silent captain took his place in the port lifeboat, the sailors pushed it away from the ship with their oars and then pulled around under the stern to join Mackey and the rest of the crew, who were rowing strongly for the Dartmouth shore.

Behind them, the blazing *Mont Blanc*, caught on the flood tide, continued to drift slowly across the harbour toward Pier 6 and doomed Richmond.

"Oh my, will you look at that now."

"What happened? Did you see what happened?"

"Now that's what I'd call a real fire."

"Bobby, stop pickin' ya nose, will ya. Look, see the pretty flames?"

"A thing like that could be dangerous. Shouldn't something be done?"

"Aw, come on. Let's go."

"Them sailors is gettin' off her quick enough."

"Can't say I blame 'em."

"Stop doin' that I say, Bobby. You won't stay. I'll take ya home right now."

"Has anyone called the fire department?"

"How the hell should I know? I've got my own troubles."

"Hey, she's drifting in closer all the time."

"...and what's the navy doing about it? Nothing. Sitting on their arse."

"Jee-sus!"

"Did ya hear that, did ya? Another of them barrels went off."

"Oil, that what it is. Ain't gonna be easy to put out, that ain't."

"Let's go up apiece. Get a better view from there."

"Bobby!"

"So what? So we'll be late, that's what! Come on!"

Unaware of any danger to them, men, women, and children on Campbell Road paused to gather in excited groups against the parapet and look out over the dockside below them toward the burning ship, and passing trams slowed to a crawl so that passengers and crews could better take in the drama.

From vantage points on the sidewalk or at upper windows of the wooden houses, there were more interested spectators in the streets, running across the slope of the hill that led up to the old earthworks and open ground of Fort Needham. On the waterfront, in the shipyards, and on the jetties close by, the men stopped work to watch the blaze, and aboard the cargo steamers and tugs that crowded the wharves from the dry dock to Pier 9, the cry, "Ship on fire!" brought the seamen from all quarters at the double to line the decks.

Downtown, on Barrington and Granville Streets, a few of the housewives out early to be first in the shops noticed the dark smoke rising over the north end of the city, but thought little of it as they hurried about their business. As typewriters began to chatter and the new date was entered in countless ledgers throughout the commercial quarter, the first wave of children converging on school, those in the upper grades, ebbed to only a few, gloved and muffled against the cold and preoccupied with excuses for their lateness.

En route for Mr. Strickland's Academy on Morris Street, nine-year-old Trevor Frowd reflected sadly that it was unlikely that his teacher would be very sympathetic when he explained that a vain search for his spaniel was the reason for his turning up in the middle of morning prayers. But what else could a fellow do when his best friend had disappeared? The hunt for his dog had taken all his time since breakfast and had led him to every conceivable hiding place in and around his home in the dockyard, where his father was serving as an engineer captain in the Royal Navy. In fact, he had been so intent on finding the dog that everything else around him had gone unnoticed and unheeded so that, as the tram that carried him toward school rattled along Lockman Street, he was totally unaware of the fire in the Narrows.

When William Fowlie, the night shift over, stepped out of the warmth of the Dennis Building and onto the sidewalk, he found that the chill air quickly dispelled his feeling of tiredness. He pulled the collar of his overcoat up around his neck and waited for Brady and Henderson, two of his colleagues, to join him. It was such a fine morning that when they were assembled the three young men decided to walk home and so, together, they strode briskly up the hill toward the Citadel.

Fowlie had only been in Halifax since February when, on completing his training as an operator, he had been sent out from England, but already he had developed a great attachment for the place. He liked the work to which he had been assigned, and he found in the struggling city a peculiar beauty which, he felt, was never so evident than on a morning such as this, when the sun sparkled on the water of the harbour and the walls of the hilltop fortress were bathed in a clear golden light. "It's good to be alive on a day like this," he thought.

When they reached Wellington Barracks, the trio stopped and talked for a while and then they said their goodbyes and split up. Brady and Henderson, who boarded together, still had some way to go, but for Fowlie, his lodgings on Russell Street were only a few blocks away.

When he reached the house, and after he had washed and briefly scanned the morning paper, he sat down to a late breakfast with his landlady, Mrs. Clark, and her daughter.

"If you didn't get it dirty every five minutes, I wouldn't have to keep washing your face!" exclaimed Bessie Fraser as her son William squirmed under the flannel. For the Fraser family the first meal of the day was over, and both William and Hattie were eager to get out of the house and play, but their mother had refused them permission. Next door and in the home opposite, the youngsters were stricken with diphtheria—victims of a minor epidemic which had spread through Dartmouth and Halifax—and Mrs. Fraser dreaded the possibility of either of her elder children wandering too close to the infected houses, thereby laying themselves open to the killer disease.

"Now if you are both good," she announced, "I'll take you out myself in a little while, but first I've got to light the kitchen stove. William, you come and help me chop some kindling, and Hattie, look at your book and listen to your baby brother for me, eh?"

Hattie was thrilled at being given such a responsibility, and when her mother, followed by her brother proudly carrying the chopper, had gone down to the basement, she tiptoed into the parlour and looked over the edge of the pram. She was more than a little disappointed to find the youngest member of the Fraser household snugly tucked up and fast asleep.

At the time when the *Imo* was manoeuvring her way through the ships anchored in Bedford Basin, the oceangoing tug *Stella Maris* left the dry dock wharf towing two heavily laden and unwieldy scows. Her destination was the Basin, and Captain Horatio Brannan accordingly shaped his course at an angle across the harbour to take up his correct station on the Dartmouth side of the channel.

The tug and barges were in midstream above Pier 9 when Brannan saw the *Imo* bearing down on him fast and in what was, for an outward bound vessel, the wrong water. Steaming as she was, within minutes she would be on him, but if the pilot of the relief ship corrected his course as the captain of the tug felt certain he was bound to do, the *Stella Maris* could still continue her crossing in safety.

Then the Norwegian let go two short blasts on her whistle.

"The bloody fool! He's taking her down against Dartmouth. We'll be across her bows," cursed Brannan. "Go about."

Slowly the tug swung round until she was headed back toward the Halifax shore, and as the scows sluggishly turned behind her, the *Imo* pounded past and on down the harbour.

Walter Brannan, first mate on the *Stella Maris*, had joined his father on the bridge when the collision occurred. They saw the *Imo* pull away from the damaged *Mont Blanc* and, almost immediately, the fire break out on the Frenchman's forward deck. As the flames took hold to boil skyward and the crew of the freighter let go their lifeboats, the skipper ordered his son to get a hose rigged in the stern of the tug, and added, "I'm going to anchor these scows, and then let's get over there in a hurry and do something about that blaze."

Anchoring the barges close inshore took time, but when it was done the *Stella Maris* raced back down the harbour toward the *Mont Blanc*, which was now only a few yards off Pier 6 and drifting closer with every second.

Immediately after he received a report of the collision and the condition of the French ship, Captain Garnett left his quarters and went up onto the bridge of HMS *Highflyer*. Although he was not aware of the nature of the cargo carried by the *Mont Blanc*, on seeing the extent of the fire he had no doubt whatever that the situation was potentially a dangerous one, and he sent a message to Acting Commander T. K. Triggs, RN, to join him on the bridge.

At first Garnett was not at all sure just how the cruiser could be of practical assistance quickly, as all her boats of any useful size were away at the time. The steam cutter and sailing pinnace had only just landed a party of stokers for exercise on the Dartmouth shore under Engineer Commander Hopkyns, and had not yet returned; but then he saw, up ahead, the ship's whaler pulling back from HMCS *Niobe*, to where she had earlier been dispatched on routine business.

When Commander Triggs reported to him, the captain said, "I'm not at all happy about that fire, Tom. I want you to get an officer to go down at once in the whaler and see if anything can be done about it. If he can get on board the Frenchman and drop her anchor, that will at least keep her off the pier. Failing that, tell him he's to try and get the other ship under control and well out of the way."

Triggs nodded. "If it's all right with you, sir, I'll go myself," he said.

"Excuse me, sir, but I'd be very happy to accompany the commander if he thinks I could be of help," volunteered Lieutenant James Rayward Ruffles, RNR, who had been standing close by on the bridge and so had overheard the captain's orders.

"Glad to have you along, Ruffles."

"Very well. Carry on, Commander." Garnett dismissed the two men, and they left the bridge and went down to the whaler, which had now come alongside.

There was muted grumbling amongst the boat's crew when, having just pulled back from the *Niobe*, they found themselves ordered away again, but once Triggs and the young lieutenant were seated in the stern sheets, the oarsmen struck out strongly for the *Mont Blanc*, drifting some three-quarters of a mile up-channel.

As they sped through the calm but ice-cold water, neither the two officers nor any of the five sailors in the whaler—Leading Seaman Claude Rushen, Able Seaman James Dowling, Able Seaman Samuel David Prewer, Able Seaman Joseph Murphy, and Able Seaman William Becker—had any idea of the terrible danger involved in their mission.

From the bridge of the cruiser, Captain Garnett followed the boat's progress with interest. Ignorant of the explosives stored in the holds of the blazing freighter, he could not have foreseen that of the seven men he had sent up across the harbour, only one would live to see the day out.

Despite the speed with which it had been dispatched, the whaler was not in time to prevent the *Mont Blanc* from striking Pier 6. When the *Highflyer*'s boat arrived on the scene, the French vessel had already slammed up against the jetty and had set fire to the wooden pilings and pier sheds. The *Stella Maris* was alongside, Captain Brannan and his crew vainly attempting to combat the roaring inferno with the jet from their single hose.

Triggs ordered the whaler into the side of the tug, which he boarded so as to confer with her captain. Brannan met him on deck and shouted above the noise of the fire, "We're doing no good with what we've got here. Might as well try to put hell out with spit!"

The commander nodded his agreement. Seen close to, it was immediately clear to him that the fire on board was a job for experts, and one which would take every available navy fire appliance to bring under control.

"Best thing we can do is to get her into the channel again," he replied. "If we tow her off the pier, the fire department can cope with that and stop the flames spreading onshore. There'll be other tugs on their way by now with proper equipment. They can best tackle the ship out in the stream."

As Brannan and Triggs worked out their plan of action, the steam pinnace of HMCS *Niobe*, sent from the depot ship to render assistance under the command of Bo'sun Albert Mattison, RCN, came alongside the *Stella Maris*.

"Billy" Brock had had no time for his books. All thoughts of cramming had been banished when someone looking out from Study 8 had seen the great cloud rising up from the Narrows and had shouted the exciting news.

With the other juniors, Brock pressed around the window of the ground-floor room. At first they could clearly see the *Mont Blanc* as she drifted, burning, across the harbour, but as she got closer inshore, she was lost from sight behind the tall building of the Acadia Sugar Refinery that stood between the college and Pier 6, almost at the water's edge. All that was then visible was the billowing smoke through which, every now and then, a mass of fire could be seen rising.

From the study, the cadets could make out a throng of spectators on the flat roof of the refinery. "Lucky devils!" said one boy. "They've got a grandstand view."

Then the first warning gong was sounded, and reluctantly the juniors dragged themselves away from the spectacle to double along to their gunroom on the west side of the building, to brush up for "divisions" and the morning inspection.

Through a large window in the chemistry and mechanics laboratory, Senior Cadet Mackenzie followed the drama intently with Chief Petty Officer William King, one of the instructors at the college. As they gazed northward, with King, the taller of the two, standing behind Mackenzie with his hands on the cadet's shoulders, they saw the flames shoot higher and higher, and the whaler pull away from *Highflyer*, its oars beating the water in perfect and urgent rhythm.

With Francis Mackey directing their course, the two lifeboats from the *Mont Blanc* made for a beach a quarter of a mile up on the Dartmouth shore, above which, on rising ground, lay a small wood.

Everyone in the boats knew that at any minute the ship they had abandoned would explode with unimaginable force, and the men at the oars strained and sweated in a frenzied race for cover.

They were nearing the beach when Mackey turned and saw that the tug *Hilford*, coming down from Bedford Basin, was almost directly across from them in mid-channel and only about two hundred yards away. On the deck of the tug, he could make out the figure of a man he knew very well, Lieutenant Commander J. A. Murray, RNVR, sea transport officer on the staff of Rear Admiral Chambers, the port convoy officer.

The pilot stood up in the lifeboat and waved his arms to attract Murray's attention, but the naval officer's eyes were on the burning *Mont Blanc*.

"Go away, go away!" roared Mackey, cupping a hand to his mouth. "That ship is going to explode!"

When Murray gave no signs of having seen or heard him, the pilot waved and called out again. This time it seemed to him that he was spotted from the tug, but he could not be sure, for, almost as he repeated his warning, the *Hilford* turned a little to starboard and the commander was lost from sight.

Immediately after the lifeboats ground up onto the beach, the men in them leapt ashore. "Make for the trees," shouted Le Medec and, scrambling over the shingle, pushing and falling over one another in their terror, the crew ran for shelter in the wood.

Lieutenant Commander James Murray had put to sea in the *Hilford* at 7:30 that morning. As sea transport officer, he was responsible for liaison between the port convoy office and all the merchant ships that put into Halifax to be escorted across the Atlantic. He was excellently suited for this work, as prior to active service with the RNVR he had been master of the liner *Empress of Britain*, and therefore could foresee, and so tactfully forestall, likely points of friction between the highly individualistic and often stubbornly independent officers of the merchant navy, and those entrusted with their safety.

With a convoy due to sail the next day, Murray was anxious to clear up, well before the final briefing, any outstanding queries among the captains of those vessels now anchored in Bedford Basin that were scheduled to join it.

He had another and more personal reason for making his rounds unusually early that day. The morning before he had been on board the Union-Castle steamer *Corfu Castle* discussing the convoy arrangements with her chief officer, L. P. Wilkie, and as he was leaving he paused outside the saloon where the rest of the officers were at breakfast to sniff the air and remark involuntarily, "What a lovely smell of kippers!"

It had not taken much persuasion from the chief officer to get Murray to join the others at the table, and during the course of the meal he had said to the captain, who was seated opposite him, "My wife will be so jealous when I tell her about this. We've not had a kipper since we left Liverpool, and they're one of the things we really miss being out here."

The captain immediately offered to give him a few pairs from the stores. At first embarrassed, Murray had finally accepted gratefully, but had added that as he was then going to visit other ships in the Basin he would rather collect the fish the following morning and surprise his wife with them at breakfast.

So it was that at 8:40 A.M., five minutes before the *Imo* ploughed into the *Mont Blanc*, Murray dropped back into his tug from the deck of the *Corfu Castle* with the neatly parcelled kippers under his arm.

He saw the smoke from the fire as the *Hilford* entered the northwestern end of the Narrows and, concerned, he ordered her captain to make all speed down channel.

Whether the commander saw Mackey waving from the lifeboat or heard his shouted warning it is impossible to say, as Murray was not to live to tell his story; but it is clear from the evidence available that, when still some distance away, he identified the burning freighter. He had earlier that week been notified by New York to expect the *Mont Blanc*, and he had been advised of the deadly cargo she carried. At the moment of collision, the only other persons in Halifax to share this knowledge with him were Rear Admiral Chambers and Chief Examining Officer Wyatt and his staff.

On realizing the imminence of a terrible disaster, Murray urged the *Hilford* toward Pier 9 and his office, from where, if there was still time, he could telephone a general warning.

The number of spectators on the slope of Fort Needham hill, along Campbell Road, and on the waterfront had grown steadily with every passing minute, but it was not until some time after the *Mont Blanc* had struck and ignited the pier that anyone put in an alarm call.

Almost at the same moment that Constant Upham, whose grocery store was across the street from the blaze, finally got around to telephoning the fire department, some other citizen rang the warning bell in a nearby fire hall tower, and its urgent message was relayed across the town by the other towers that made up the old fire alarm system.

The response of Fire Chief Edward Condon was immediate. The Halifax fire department had thirteen pieces of apparatus, but of these only one was motorized: the *Patricia*, a sixty-seven horse power American LaFrance that had been commissioned in 1912. On Upham's call, her five-man crew was mustered, and the engine sent roaring from the station with Condon and Deputy Chief Brunt following close behind in a car.

As the firemen raced to the scene, sailors from the *Niobe*'s steam pinnace, acting on Lieutenant Commander Triggs's orders, boarded the *Mont Blanc* to secure a 5-inch hawser in her stern so that the *Stella Maris* could tow her away on a short line from the pier. They climbed slowly up the port ladder amidships, left dangling when the ship was

Train dispatcher Vincent Coleman

abandoned, arching themselves away from the metal plates, which were now so hot from the fire raging within that where they touched the sea they hissed furiously and the water steamed.

When all was ready, the tug, with Triggs still aboard, went ahead gently to take up the slack, while the whaler from *Highflyer* stood off a yard or so. The towline snapped taut, but the freighter did not move and it was obvious to everyone that the hawser was not strong enough to stand the strain. Brannan took the *Stella Maris* back in alongside.

"I'll have to use a ten-inch," he explained. "That should do it."

"Right," agreed Triggs, and then, deciding that everything possible was being done so far as the *Mont Blanc* was concerned, he turned to the bo'sun from the depot ship and ordered, "Mr. Mattison, you and your men stay with the Captain and get the hawser secured. I'm going over to the other ship to see what can be done there."

The *Imo* still lay out in the harbour with the way off her, seemingly undamaged but helpless, lazily turning with the tide. There was no movement to be seen on her decks and it was as if, in an instant, she had become a ghost ship.

Triggs signalled to the whaler to come in for him. He dropped down into the stern sheets again to stand beside Lieutenant Ruffles, and then ordered the boat pulled toward the lifeless Norwegian vessel.

Edith O'Connell and her sister watched the fire for a time from the window of their home. Upstairs, their grandmother was ill in bed, and the girls' mother and an aunt who was staying with them were too busy about the house to join them. On the floor of the front room, their two-year-old brother, Herman, played quietly by himself. After a while their Aunt Helena, who lived just around the corner from them, called with her daughter, Mary, and tried to persuade Mrs. O'Connell to come out and see the blaze.

"No, Helena, you know I can't leave mother, and anyway I wouldn't take young Herman out there, it's too cold for him. The girls can go with you, though, if they want to."

Chattering excitedly, Edith and Lulu put on their coats and then, hand in hand, went out with their aunt and cousin across Campbell Road to stand up against the parapet overlooking Pier 6.

Murray took the four feet of water that still separated the *Hilford* from the shore with a running jump and then, without pausing, sprinted away to his office.

Above Pier 9 lay Richmond Station and the freight yards of the Canadian Government Railway. When the commander saw a sailor approaching him along the jetty, he pulled up for a moment. Breathlessly he ordered the bewildered man away at the double to warn everyone in the vicinity of the yards to get clear, and then he ran on again.

In the outer office of the railway yardmaster, two hundred yards away from where the *Mont Blanc* lay burning, chief clerk William Lovett and train dispatcher Vincent Coleman were discussing the fire when the door was thrown open and the sailor sent by Murray burst in.

"Everybody out!" he shouted. "Run like hell! Commander says that bloody ship is loaded with tons of explosives and she'll blow up for certain." Then he was gone again and the door slammed shut behind him.

For a second neither man moved and the only sound in the office was the ticking of the clock on the wall and the muted roar of the billowing flames outside. Then Lovett leapt for the telephone and got through to the CGR terminal agent's office on Cornwallis Street.

"Mr. Dustan? This is Bill Lovett. There's a steamer on fire against Pier 6 and we've just been told by the navy that she's carrying explosives and is likely to go up any minute...Right... No, he's not here at the moment...Just Coleman and me...Yes, we're clearing out now."

Lovett and Coleman made for the door together. They had left the office and were making their way across the tracks when the dispatcher stopped and turned back.

"What do you think you're doing?" demanded Lovett. "We've got to keep moving."

"I've just remembered. There are trains due in shortly. I must telegraph through to Rockingham and Truro to have them hold everything up."

"But Vince, it's too dangerous. You heard what the sailor said. It could be we've only got a minute or two left. Anyone in the office wouldn't stand a chance, and you're a married man with a family to think of."

"Bill, I know that, but someone's got to stop those trains. There could be hundreds killed if not."

Before his companion could say anything further, Coleman ran back toward the office. Once there, he seated himself at his desk, reached for the telegraph key, and began to tap out his message.

At five minutes past nine by the town clock, Lillian Atkins in the Dominion Textile factory turned to the girl working at the machine next to her and sighed, "My, this morning seems long."

As the big hand on the clock moved slowly through the next minute, little Edith O'Connell and her sister craned forward for a better view...Captain Aimé Le Medec ordered a roll call of his crew..."Billy" Brock was idly glancing at a newspaper in the junior gunroom, and Cadet Mackenzie and CPO King were at the laboratory window. The *Patricia* and Fire Chief Condon and his deputy had almost reached the head of Pier 6...William Fowlie was finishing breakfast...the *Highflyer*'s whaler was passing under the stern of the *Mont Blanc*, whilst the larger hawser was swung upward from the deck of the *Stella Maris*. Over in the basement of her Dartmouth home, Mrs. Fraser collected together the kindling she had chopped and passed the wood to her son, who packed it into a box...Trevor Frowd, who had left the tram at the corner of Barrington Street and Spring Garden Road, was halfway between the tram stop and school... at his desk in Richmond, Vincent Coleman just managed to complete his warning message with "...munition ship on fire in the harbour—Goodbye"—and then the sixty seconds were past. Time had run out for Halifax.

At 9:06 A.M. precisely, the *Mont Blanc* blew up.

CHAPTER FIVE

UP FROM THE WATER'S EDGE

In one-fiftieth of a second the French ship vanished in a searing ball of flaming gases. With a thundering, staccato roar the blast waves from the exploding chemicals struck out at Halifax and Dartmouth with the violence of a hundred typhoons. The earth shook and the bed of the harbour was split open.

Along the waterfront wooden piers erupted and the sea boiled. Large ships were stripped of funnels and superstructure; smaller vessels disappeared entirely. Heavy cranes and masses of debris were flung high into the air to twist and turn like blown leaves, caught up in a nightmare whirlwind. Wooden buildings were punched away, and those of concrete crumbled and fell. In an instant acres of dockland were levelled and wasted.

With a scream of rending metal, a bridge spanning the railway was swept away and the tracks were plucked from the earth, bent and corkscrewed. Freight and passenger cars were hurled around the yards, thrown up onto the road and out across the harbour. Station walls cracked and burst in, roofs collapsed, and engine sheds and offices were ripped away from their foundations.

The shank of one of *Mont Blanc*'s anchors at Regatta Point, 1918. The shaft weighed half a ton and was hurled over the city for two miles before falling out of the sky.

Up from the water's edge and into the town raced the air wall of destruction. Roads trembled into a thousand running fissures; tramlines buckled; trees were uprooted; telegraph poles snapped like matches; and the overhead power cables, torn from their supports, whip-cracked in the air, sparking fiercely. Close to the explosion centre, street after street was obliterated with savage force as churches, schools, shops, factories, and houses alike caved in or burst into clouds of flying wreckage.

On and on sped the hideous blast, losing strength with every yard but still of incalculable force. From those buildings that did not fall it took almost every window, pounded them into vicious dagger blades and needle splinters, and swept these fragments along with it in a swirling blizzard of shattered glass. Then, in Halifax, it struck the bulk of Citadel Hill and the granite walls of the fortress. The slopes shuddered and the walls trembled, but the blow was deflected upward to waste its strength in the air and around the base of the hill, to close up again on the other side and pour over the South End; but now, dispersed and weakened, it was as but a dying hurricane.

As the air was pressed out with such tremendous force so, almost immediately, it was sucked in again to fill the vacuum that the explosion had created, eddying the glass and other still-airborne debris backward, sucking nails from woodwork to fly like shrapnel, dragging down walls and buildings which had withstood the initial shock, and bowling hundreds of tons of wreckage before it.

Fires, started either by the millions of cubic feet of gas that had ignited and blazed momentarily in the air in the wake of the blast, or by the live coals from hundreds of wrecked stoves that had been scattered over the collapsed wooden houses, had already taken hold in Richmond. Then, as the pressure subsided, the sky rained further destruction and torment.

Rocks, many of them huge, which had been scooped up from the sea bed and hurled into the air by the explosion, now crashed back to earth, and with them descended a shower of more than three thousand tons of red-hot metal fragments— all that was left of the *Mont Blanc*. Among these fragments, an anchor shank from the freighter, almost intact and weighing half a ton, dropped into the woods across the Northwest Arm two miles from the explosion, and her forward gun, its barrel melted away, fell into Albro Lake a mile or more behind Dartmouth.

When the sky emptied, even then hell was not yet finished with the stricken towns.

Following the explosions came the fury of the sea. As it rushed in to fill the chasm that had opened in the harbour bed, a monstrous wave, thirteen feet high, reared up in a gigantic bore to foam outwards at incredible speed.

It roared over the water, an immense hissing, spurning torrent, to tear steamers and warships from their moorings, and to roll tugs and light craft into itself and carry them along until they were crashed down far inshore, when it deluged the dockside and broken piers and raced knee-deep into the streets high up on the slopes above.

As quickly as it had flooded, the water drained away again, and the wave passed on down the channel to burst over McNabs Island and then billow out into the Atlantic, where some hours later and many miles out at sea, it lifted a merchant ship with such force that her captain thought she had struck a mine.

When the wave had gone, and the air wall and the earth tremor had fled out into the province to set church bells swinging and booming in towns more than sixty miles distant, a widening column of smoke and burnt-out gases rose for three miles into the sky above the North End. It hung there for many minutes,

"A widening column of smoke and burnt-out gases rose for three miles into the sky above the North End."

turning from black to grey and then to cotton-wool white, and it looked for all the world like some enormous, mutated mushroom.

The blast tore down the Acadia Sugar Refinery and spouted the workmen, who had gathered on its roof to watch the fire, out over the city.

Killing and mutilating, it scythed through the spectators on the waterfront and on Campbell Road, and it swept up Edith O'Connell and tossed the child into the air. She knew she was being carried upward in a dizzy, sickening spiral, but she could see nothing, for the flash of the explosion had blinded her. Up and up she went, twisting and turning, her clothes ripped away from her body until she was naked. She wanted to cry out in her terror but she could not open her mouth, and then, with a final somersault, she plummeted back to earth.

She fell on the wreckage down by the water's edge, and as she landed, an agonizing pain swept through her body. She gave a single piercing scream and then passed out.

Edith was still unconscious when the towering wave broke over her and flung her in a flurry of shattered wood and twisted metal further back on the wharf. For a long time after the flood had receded around her, she lay soaked and still. Then, struggling back to consciousness, the seven-year-old girl stirred. Her eyelids flickered open and immediately she was seized with terror again, for she still could not see. She put up her hand to touch her face and it came away warm and sticky with blood. For a while she did not attempt to move, but lay shivering and sobbing uncontrollably. Pitifully she wondered what had happened to her and where she was, but she could remember nothing. She knew only that she wanted her mother and she called for her, *"Momma! Momma!"* and when her mother did not come, *"Lulu! Lulu!"*

But there was nobody to hear her and she faded back into unconsciousness.

When she came to, much of the wreckage around her was on fire and she could feel the heat. Instinctively she knew she must get away and she tried to lift herself up, only to fall back with a moan when the pain surged over her once more. One arm and a leg were smashed and broken, her face and head were badly cut, and her body was bruised and lacerated.

As the heat grew more intense, Edith desperately tried again to move. With a great effort, and biting her lip against the pain, she rolled over onto her stomach and then, with her uninjured arm and leg, her broken limbs trailing uselessly, she clawed and pushed her way blindly inch by inch over the debris.

It took her more than a quarter of an hour to drag herself in this way twelve feet, and then her groping fingers touched a face. It was cold and wet and she could feel a thick moustache. She spoke to the man. He did not answer, and she thought that he was asleep and tried to wake him, but when she could not she knew that he was dead. Frightened but desperate, she pulled herself up and over the corpse, only to come up against another body and then another. Sick and mute with horror, she crawled on for a few more minutes but then she could go no further. Lifting her arm to wave feebly, she cried out, "Momma! Momma! I'm here, I'm here."

But her mother could not hear her, for she was dead, as was everyone else who had been in the house on Campbell Road or had stood with Edith at the parapet—Lulu, Herman, Mary, Aunt Helena, everyone—all were killed by the blast that had burst in from the sea. Of the O'Connells, only Edith had survived, and she lay on the wharf alone and in a dark world of pain, crying out for help. Mercifully, the child soon lost consciousness again.

When the *Mont Blanc* exploded, the walls of the naval college shook and cracked open, and its rooms were filled with falling plaster and blown glass, but the building did not collapse.

Cadet Brock, bent over his newspaper, had the right side of his face to the window of the gunroom. The blast threw him to the floor with slivers of glass embedded in his right cheek, and he lay there dazed and bleeding, his ears straining against the terrifying roaring sound that filled the room.

For a few moments he lay there, feeling rather than seeing that there were others around him on the floor. Then he scrambled to his feet. Although their gunroom was on the west side of the college and thus had been shielded from much of the

Wreckage as viewed from Campbell Road looking north.

blast by the rooms behind it, it was a shambles. Most of the juniors had been injured by the flying glass and many were bleeding freely, but luckily no one had been seriously hurt.

When they had all picked themselves up, they rushed wildly from the room, over the door that had been wrenched from its hinges, down the hall through a powder mist of plaster, and out onto the lawn in front of the building. Here, with one accord, they threw themselves face down on the grass and covered their heads with their arms.

Red-hot rivets and other small pieces of debris fell among them and ploughed into the earth, missing the prostrate bodies by inches. Then, with a crash, a larger section of the *Mont Blanc*'s boiler hit the roof of the college and ripped downward through the upper floor into Study 8, where it shattered the master's dais and splintered the empty desks.

As he lay on the lawn, Brock could hear the fragments falling around him and others ricocheting with a shrill whine off the building and the concrete roadway, and he was convinced that the German fleet was bombarding Halifax. "It can't be long before they get the range of the college," he thought.

But then, suddenly, the rain of wreckage stopped and except for a distant crackle of flames it was very quiet. After a while the junior cadets got up from the grass and, stunned, utterly bewildered, and without anyone to give them orders, they ran off.

"Billy" Brock made for the dockyard north gate without knowing why or what he would do when he got there. The bombardment seemed to be over, at least for the moment, and perhaps at the gate he would find someone to tell him what was happening. If not, perhaps he would go into the city. He did not really know, but he ran because everyone was running, and the direction he had chosen seemed as good as any other.

The northern entrance to the dockyard was just above the point where the railway ran into North Street Station, and the roadway through the gate was carried over the tracks by a bridge to join the lower end of Campbell Road. When Brock reached it, there seemed to be no one about; even the sentry box had been deserted, so he ran on through the gate. Then he stopped dead in his tracks.

Sprinting across the dockyard he had seen that most of the buildings in it had been badly damaged, with roofs and windows gone and walls leaning at crazy angles, but this was nothing compared to the devastation outside. To his left he could see that the massive glass canopy of North Street Station had fallen in onto the platforms below. The tracks were broken and littered with wreckage, and the sidings were heaped with smashed and upturned rolling stock; a locomotive lay on its side wrapped in a cocoon of belching steam. But northward, beyond the bridge, the scene was even more terrible, almost total obliteration. A few buildings still stood, and here and there a tottering wall, but for the most part the north end of the city appeared as a wilderness, a vast burning scrapyard, over which hung an enormous billowing cloud of smoke.

The laboratory on the east side of the naval college took a great deal of the full force of the blast. The window before Kenneth Mackenzie and CPO King disintegrated into a million pieces, and together they were hurled back, their hands, faces, and eyes riddled with jagged glass. The floor heaved, the ceiling cracked and gaped open, and the walls bulged inward.

Mackenzie was stunned for a moment, and when he regained consciousness he was in terrible pain. His face, horribly cut, was coated with blood and plaster, and he was blind, his eyes thick with splinters. Around him he could hear jars of chemicals on the laboratory shelves, affected in some way by the blast, popping and exploding, and the chief petty officer groaning in agony.

"Oh God, I can't see! I'm blind! Oh, I can't stand it. Help me, help me!"

Somehow Mackenzie got to his feet and felt his way over to the sink. He searched around with his hands until he found a towel, which he soaked under the tap. Then, dropping to his knees, he crawled toward his companion, guided by the piteous cries for help. Forcing King's hands away from his torn face, he bathed it gently, and when he had done that he laid the wet and bloody towel over the man's sightless eyes. Then he was engulfed by a great blackness, and he toppled over and knew nothing more for a long time.

It seemed to William Fowlie that everything in the room had suddenly come to life as the furniture whirled around him in a wild dance. First he felt himself thrust forward hard against the table, his spine curving under the pressure, then he was lifted off his feet and slammed in the opposite direction into a door that fell on top of him.

He could not see across the room, for the air was thick with plaster and flying wreckage, but he saw a wall behind him bend and fall in to block the way out to the hall. Choking and coughing, he lay on the floor with a dull ache in his chest and legs. He made an attempt to push the heavy door off his body, but he found that moving made the pain much worse so he gave up trying.

When the cloud of plaster had settled, he saw Mrs. Clark and her daughter lying across from him, partially buried by pieces of their shattered home. At first he thought they were dead, for they lay very still, but then, to his relief, they both sat up, his landlady brushing the dust out of her hair.

The women were at his side the moment they had struggled free from the rubble, and Fowlie marvelled to see how calm they were. Practical as always, Mrs. Clark lost no time in discussing or questioning what had happened. Helped by her daughter, she lifted the door away and then asked, "Are you hurt badly, Mr. Fowlie?"

"No, I don't think so, but I've got a bit of pain in my chest and I don't think I can stand up. What about you? Are you both all right?"

"Oh, don't you worry about us, we're fine. A bit bruised, that's all, thank God. Now you lie still for a minute while I have a look around outside and see what's what."

Lifting her skirt a little, she picked her way delicately over the wreckage and went out through the doorway leading to the garden at the rear of the house. The leaded glass door itself, closed tightly only a little while earlier, had now disappeared. In less than five minutes she was back.

"Oh, it's terrible. Just about every house in the street is down. Poor souls," was her only comment on the disaster. Then she said briskly, "We must get you out of here quickly. I've been around to the front door, or where it used to be, more like. The

The burnt-out shell of the Dominion Textile Company's factory on Robie Street. The floor of the spinning room gave way in the blast, sending tons of concrete and machinery crashing down on the workers below.

roof's gone, and the stairs are hanging away from the wall. That's bad enough, but the hall stove has spilled over and the coals have set light to the wood."

Between them, the two women got Fowlie to his feet and helped him outside into the garden, where gently they laid him down again on the lawn.

What little was left of the house next door was blazing fiercely and, long before the fire from the overturned hall stove had a chance to develop, the flames from it licked across to take hold instantly amid the ruins of what had once been a bedroom.

Suddenly, and for the first time that morning, Mrs. Clark was no longer calm. She covered her cheeks with her hands in alarm and her eyes widened. "My silver teapot! I must save that," she exclaimed, and before her daughter could stop her, she rushed back into her burning home.

Lillian Atkins turned to the girl working at the machine next to her and sighed, "My, this morning seems long." The next thing she knew was that she was on her back on the floor, her right arm, which she had flung up instinctively to protect her eyes, her face, and her head, cut and bleeding.

The Dominion Textile Company's cotton factory had taken the full force of the blast wave, and the stone building trembled as though it were made of straw. Workers fell where they stood as if poleaxed, stunned by the immense concussion. The dirty panes of glass in the tall windows, many of them already broken and stuffed with rags, fractured into minute particles and poured in over the machines, and first cracks and then great holes appeared in the outer walls. The shock rippled the reinforced concrete floors of the workrooms and they split open.

Terrified, Lillian lay where she had fallen and waited for the world to stop swaying. She prayed hard and earnestly, and when at last she staggered upright, she went on praying, repeating the familiar lines over and over again.

."Our Father which art in Heaven, Hallowed be thy name."

There was wreckage littered all around her and the air was full of hideous sounds. Somewhere in a far corner, a girl, racked by a bubbling cough, was crying loudly. In many places the floor of the spinning room had given way, to send tons of concrete and many of the monster machines crashing down through the building to kill and maim.

"Thy Kingdom come. Thy will be done in earth, as it is in heaven."

Lillian had no clear idea as to how she was going to get out of the factory. She did not even know if the stairs were still standing, but, clambering over broken and twisted metal and edging round the gaping holes, she worked her way toward the door. She found it very difficult at times to keep her balance, as the floor was slippery with blood. All the time she kept praying.

"Give us this day our daily bread."

She reached the doorway just as the girl who had been coughing gave a high wailing sob and then died.

The stairs were shaky and misshapen, but they had withstood the blast. Lillian was halfway down to the second floor before she realized that she was bleeding profusely from the cuts on her temples, face, and arm, but she was too numb with shock to feel any pain.

The second floor was nothing now but a narrow ledge of ragged concrete running along the four walls. Everything else had been taken down by the machines when they had fallen through from above. On the landing, a shattered pipe gushed water into the air and Lillian was drenched by it, blood and water mingling to trickle down her face like cherry soda.

"And forgive us our debts, as we forgive our debtors."

The ground floor, a scene of mangled horror, was alive with screams and desperate cries for help. "Save me! Oh Jesus, save me!"

"Won't somebody come? I'm hurt here."

"Mary! Mary!"

"My legs, my legs! I can't get out!"

"For God's sake, don't let me die!"

Lillian wanted to help, but there was nothing she could do. Her stomach retched at the terrible things she saw. Dozens of lifeless, unrecognizable forms lay crushed under the rubble and the heavy machines, and dozens more, mostly young girls and middle-aged women, were trapped by an arm or a leg, pinned down across the chest, or even buried completely except for a foot or five waving fingers. Some of the faces were twisted into savage masks of agony; others were calm and serene as if the brain behind them had accepted the approach of the end. The walls, the masses of concrete, and the machinery ran red with blood. Over against one wall some of the cotton had caught fire and the flames were spreading rapidly.

"I'm dying! Please don't let me die!"

"What are you doing up there, you bastards? I tell you, my arm's off!"

"Oh, Jesus, Jesus!"

The girl could stand it no more. She covered her ears with her hands and stumbled away down the last few steps.

"And lead us not into temptation, but deliver us from evil: For thine is the kingdom, and the power, and the glory, forever. Amen...Amen...Amen."

And then she was out of the building and running across Robie Street.

Lieutenant Commander Triggs was killed instantly. So were the sailors from the *Niobe*, most of them whilst hoisting the larger towline onto the deck of the *Mont Blanc*, the others in the steam pinnace when it disintegrated. In the same instant, Bo'sun Albert Mattison died with Captain Brannan and eighteen others of the *Stella Maris*.

At the moment of the explosion, Walter Brannan was leaning over the open hatch on the forward deck of the tug, and he was blown headlong into the hold, and although the *Stella Maris* was almost totally destroyed, and carried hundreds of yards before finally being driven ashore, the first mate received only minor injuries.

As Triggs was killed by the blast, the *Highflyer*'s whaler, by some fluke, was lifted intact thirty feet into the air and, with most of the crew still clinging on grimly, hurled across the channel toward Dartmouth.

The boat hit the sea again hard and stove in its keel. Seconds before it struck, however, Able Seaman William Becker had spun himself over the side, and so managed to fall clear by a yard or more.

The ice-cold water of the harbour closed over him and he felt himself sinking deeper and deeper. Then the sea seemed to go mad around him, and he was caught up in the midst of a furious swirling motion like that of a whirlpool. Round and round he spun in the vortex, all the time being sucked further and further down.

His lungs were a burning pain in his chest and he was near to passing out, when the whirlpool died away as suddenly as it had been created, and he shot to the surface.

After he had greedily gulped in air and recovered his senses, Becker looked around him. It was difficult to see very far for the thick smoke and vapours of stinking gas that hung everywhere, and through which descended clouds of black smuts. After a while, though, he made out the whaler, lying some way off and half-submerged, and then he saw, beyond the boat and swimming toward it, three men whom he recognized as Lieutenant Ruffles and Able Seamen Prewer and Murphy, and he struck out to join them.

By now his body was numb and blue with cold, and his strength was ebbing fast, so he swam slowly, and long before he was halfway to the whaler, the other men had reached it. But when they caught hold of the gunwale, it capsized, and Prewer was struck on the head and went under with the boat, and neither came up again.

Becker trod water and was about to call out to Ruffles and Murphy, when the smoke and fumes closed in around him and they were lost from sight. He knew that his only chance now was to try and reach the nearer Dartmouth shore, but he doubted he could make it. With every second he was getting noticeably weaker and he was not at all sure in which direction safety lay.

He had almost given up hope when the smoke cleared again a little, and he recognized familiar landmarks and saw he was not more than fifty yards off the Dartmouth shingle. With every stroke a torment, he started to swim again. He had not covered more than a few yards when he came upon Lieutenant Ruffles. The young officer was clinging to a drifting plank, his face and hands swollen with the cold, clearly exhausted. There was no sign of Murphy.

Summoning up extra strength, when he drew level with the Lieutenant, Becker croaked, "Can you make it to the shore, sir?"

Ruffles smiled faintly and shook his head. "No, I don't think I can manage it," he whispered, and then he let go of the plank and was swallowed up by the sea.

Despite his exertions, the Dartmouth shore seemed no nearer to Becker. Now it was even a struggle for him to stay conscious, and his legs and arms barely moved through the water.

To Bessie Fraser, in the basement of her Dartmouth home, the dull rumble seemed to come from above her. She could think of only one explanation—Hattie had somehow upset the baby carriage. Grabbing her son by the hand, she made for the short flight of steps, stumbling against the woodbox in her haste. It spilled over, and the kindling she had chopped shot out across the floor.

Mother and son were only a third of the way up from the basement when, with a deafening roar, the blast wave hit the house, and Mrs. Fraser had to fling her free arm around the banister rail in order to stay on her feet. At the same time, William cried out and clutched at her skirt.

As the building rocked under the blow, it was as though at any second 48 Queen Street would be torn from its foundations, but after a while the awful noise faded away and the house stopped shaking, and they were able to climb the rest of the steps.

In the parlour, Hattie was cowering against the table, her hair and face streaked with dust and her eyes full of fear. Strewn around her lay lengths of broken wood and lumps of plaster that had fallen from the ceiling. The two windows were gone and jagged pieces of glass protruded like darts from the walls. The pram was still upright on its wheels, but it was coated with dust and the hood was punctured and torn. Mrs. Fraser rushed over to it and looked in, and her hand flew to her mouth to stifle a scream.

The Canadian Government Railway Yards near the foot of North Street after the disaster. In the background lies the wreck of the *Imo* aground on the Dartmouth shore.

There were fragments of plaster all over the pillow, and the baby lay motionless, with eyes closed, his head and face covered with blood.

With a moan, Bessie snatched up her infant son and pressed him to her breast. "Oh, my baby! My baby is dead!" she cried. Then, followed by Hattie and William, she ran for the front door; but they could not get to it, for the passageway was heaped with wreckage. Frantically she doubled back and led the children through to the kitchen.

Here two walls leaned inward precariously and the furniture had been tossed wildly about the room. The kitchen table, at which, only a few minutes before, they had all been seated having breakfast, now lay shattered under a heavy brick chimney that had been sliced from the roof of a neighbouring house and blown in through the window.

The back door was jammed and, with the baby cradled against her, it took some time for Mrs. Fraser to wrench it open with one hand; but at last she managed it and they all raced into the yard.

Thick smoke drifted everywhere, and northward many buildings were in ruins and on fire, but the distracted mother was aware of little around her as she stood, with the two older children huddled into her legs, not knowing what to do or where to go.

She was still undecided when, a moment later, the "dead" baby opened his eyes and let out a lusty yell. Bessie was so surprised that she nearly dropped him. Disbelieving, she looked down at the tiny bundle to see that it was now moving restlessly in her arms. Both laughing and crying with relief, she sank onto her knees and, laying the baby in her lap, she gently wiped the blood away from his face with her handkerchief. Looking closer, she now saw that the only injury to the boy was a small cut above his left eye, and she choked on a sob when he stopped crying and smiled up at her.

Someone called her name, and she looked up. It was Mrs. Dickinson, a local doctor's wife. She was looking out from the small basement window of her home just across the way, and when she saw that Mrs. Fraser had spotted her, she beckoned urgently for her to come over.

"You musn't stay out in the open, my dear, it's not safe," she cried. "It's the German Zeppelins, you know, they're dropping bombs. Best bring the children in here with me." She opened the window wide.

Hattie and William clambered in first, and once she had passed the baby to Mrs. Dickinson, Bessie squeezed through the window herself and dropped into the basement.

When the crew of the *Mont Blanc* reached the thin, straggling wood, they ran on through it to the far side and then gathered in a clearing that led out onto a rough track.

With a great deal of difficulty, Captain Le Medec got the frightened sailors to line up and then he ordered the first officer to call the roll.

Glotin knew the name of every man by heart, and as he sang them out and they were acknowledged he kept a count with pencil strokes on the back of an envelope. When the roll call was finished, he totted up the strokes and then reported to Le Medec, "Everyone is here, Captain." As he spoke, the *Mont Blanc* opened up.

The ground trembled violently. Trees leapt from the earth and crashed down, whilst others snapped in two, the top halves being swept far inland. The air was filled with a flying mass of tangled branches, slime, and rocks from the sea bed, and the men from the freighter were thrown about in all directions.

Pilot Mackey was lifted up by the blast and tossed into the roots of a fallen tree. When he landed, he could feel his legs thrashing about wildly and then, for a time, everything went black.

Most of his crew were already on their feet and running away when Le Medec stood up again. He called out to them to come back, but they took no notice and ran on. Angrily the captain watched them as they fanned out across the countryside, then he checked to see if he had any injuries. Apart from a few bruises he was unhurt, but he had lost his cap and his greatcoat was in tatters, and when he started to walk he discovered that he had only one shoe. The other had been sucked off his foot by the blast and was nowhere to be seen.

As he limped past a tree that had been blown across the narrow track, he saw a man drag himself out from among the roots. It was Mackey. At first glance, though, Le Medec did not recognize him, for the pilot's face had been blackened by the fumes carried in the blast, his cheeks were scratched and bleeding, and much of his clothing had been ripped off his body.

At that moment, Leveque ran up with the news that Yves Gueguiner, one of the *Mont Blanc*'s gunners, had been seriously wounded, and the captain went with him to where the man lay groaning by a clump of bushes. He was bleeding badly.

"I think his arm is broken, and a piece of metal has gone into his back. See? There, between his shoulder blades," said the second officer.

Le Medec nodded. "We must get him to a doctor as quickly as possible."

The only other men who had not run off after the explosion were the first officer and one of the stokers, Bakily Counida, an Algerian. The captain called out to them to come over and bring the pilot with them. When they were all assembled, Glotin and the stoker picked up the wounded man, and then, led by Mackey, the party made its way slowly toward Dartmouth. They did not know it then, but barely three quarters of a mile further down the same shore lay all that was left of the ship that had rammed them.

The 5,043-ton *Imo*, seized and torn by the blast and the giant wave, had been carried across the channel and flung up onto the shingle within seconds of the explosion. Right up to the end, she had drifted aimlessly. Now she was a wreck—stripped of her superstructure and lying hard over on her starboard side, beached and flooded—and Captain Haakon From was dead.

He had been on the bridge with Pilot Hayes watching the *Mont Blanc* burn, and when the French freighter had exploded, both men had been killed instantly. Five other members of the crew died at the same time: the first officer, the bo'sun, the ship's carpenter, a coal trimmer, and the donkeyman. And all because fifty tons of coal arrived too late.

The *Imo* was not the only vessel driven onto the Dartmouth shore that morning. For more than a mile the beach was littered with battered hulls; mostly small craft, but here and there tugs and even larger ships lay either completely aground, or holed and waterlogged a few yards off.

Before the explosion, the steamer *Curaca*, newly built at a cost of $4,000,000, was tied up against Pier 8 in Halifax, waiting for a shipment of horses to add to her general cargo consigned for Britain. Above her, moored at Pier 9, The S.S. *Calonne* was also scheduled to load horses urgently needed by the armies in Europe and the Middle East for a dozen wartime duties.

When the blast struck her, the *Curaca* was shaved of her masts and funnel, and her upper works and stern were staved in. Then the freak wave tore her away from the wharf and threw her across the Narrows into Tuft's Cove, where she sank in shallow water. Of the forty-five men on board the ship at the time, only eight survived the disaster.

Damage to shipping was widespread and ran into many millions of dollars. The *Calonne*, although shielded from the full force of the explosion by the *Curaca*, was extensively damaged, and many of her crew were killed. Among the ships lying against the dry dock wharf was the *Middleham Castle*; alongside her, the tug *Douglas H. Thomas*, from the deck≠ of which John Rourke, the chief engineer, and Captain McLaine had watched the collision; and the tug *Musquash*. The *Middleham Castle*, which had been in for repairs, was now ready for sea again and would have left Halifax that day; but the blast carried away her funnel and masts, smashed all her quarters and bridge and deck erections, and broke down her decks aft of No. 2 hold, leaving her a ruin littered with the dead and the dying. The deck of the *Douglas H. Thomas* was levelled, and her steel hull ripped open so that the vessel filled with water and keeled over. The *Musquash* was riddled from stem to stern with glowing fragments of metal.

High in the dry dock, under repair, the Norwegian steamer *Hovland* was almost totally wrecked, and nearby the collier *J. A. McKee* sustained very severe damage. Altogether a dozen or more merchant ships were badly hit, and many of those which were out of the direct path of the frightful blast of air had decks and superstructure smashed by the rocks and debris that fell like rain seconds later, or were damaged when they were lifted from their moorings by the tidal wave and battered against the wharves.

When the air had cleared and the wave had passed, as far as the eye could see, the water of the harbour was thick with floating wreckage and broken, blackened bodies, and within minutes fire raged through the Richmond waterfront.

By nine o'clock on that fateful morning, six minutes before the explosion, the naval divers from *Niobe*, working on the concrete foundations of a crane bed off a dockyard pier just astern of the depot ship, were ready for their first descent. With Chief Master-at-Arms John Gammon, RCN, in charge, the detail consisted of two experienced divers, and six sailors to man the pumps and attend to the life and air lines. The air pump itself, hand operated by twin pumping wheels, stood in a wood and corrugated iron shelter not far from the ladder down which the divers would ponderously lower themselves into the cold, oily water.

For the past half-hour the party had been so engrossed in their work that they had seen and heard nothing of the drama further up the harbour.

Gammon carefully checked the divers into their suits and helmets and then, as the face glasses were tightly screwed into position, he signalled to the men in the shed to start pumping. The heavy wheels turned, and the life giving air poured through the lines and into the rubber suits.

Responding to a rap on his helmet, one of the divers got to his feet and thumped his way awkwardly over to the ladder. He descended slowly, and then the sea closed over him and he was gone, a thin line of bubbles marking his position on the bed of the harbour.

The second diver was halfway down the ladder when the explosion occurred, and he was thrown backward into the water by the concussion and sank like a stone. The two men paying

St. Joseph's School. Fifty students at the school were killed and many more injured.

out his lines died on their feet and were blown off the pier. Gammon and the sailor who was standing next to him—Able Seaman Walter Critch, RNR—were sucked up by the blast, carried for twenty feet along the wharf, and then thrown violently to the ground.

For a moment, they lay where they had fallen, dazed and badly bruised but otherwise unhurt. Then the two men scrambled to their feet again, and the master-at-arms saw to his horror that the sailors manning the diving pump had been hurled away from it, and that two of them were dead and the third obviously beyond help. The heavy, corrugated iron roof of the shelter had collapsed onto the pump, which was silent and still.

Gammon could not be certain whether or not either of the divers was still alive, but he knew that, even if by some miracle they had survived the blast, without air they would quickly suffocate. "Get to the pump!" he shouted to Critch, and then he raced for the ladder and the lifelines.

When Critch reached the shed, he found the pump undamaged but jammed under the fallen roof. Realizing that

In the streets around St. Joseph's Roman Catholic Church three hundred members of the regular congregation perished.

alone he could never completely clear the broken timbers and metal sheeting in time, he squeezed between them and the pump and heaved upward with his shoulders. Grunting and straining, he managed in this way to lift the wreckage off the wheels and then, with one hand supporting the leaning roof, he started to pump. Slowly, painfully slowly, the pistons began to suck in air again.

Operating the diving pump normally called for a team of four men, two to each wheel, working in relays to ensure a steady flow, and even then it was considered strenuous work. Now, alone, his body aching with bruises and with only one free hand, Critch found it almost impossible. Soon he was blinded by a veil of sweat and gasping for breath, but somehow he managed to keep the pump going and to maintain a trickle of air.

By the time Gammon got to the head of the ladder, the pier was being bombarded by falling debris. Red-hot fragments of metal, stones, and large pieces of concrete fell around him, but he was not hit and he hardly noticed them for the incredible sight below.

The level of the sea had fallen by more than eighteen feet in the first phase of the tidal wave, which even then was forming in a boiling mass six hundred yards further upstream. The divers, already half-suffocated despite Critch's valiant efforts, their lifelines and air hoses tangled, floundered helplessly one against the other like partners in a grotesque dance in muddy water only chest high.

The master-at-arms swung himself down the ladder. In a little while the sea would roar back into the unnatural trough with a mighty rush, and with overwhelming and killing force. Before that happened, he must somehow get the men to safety up on the pier.

He climbed down until he was just above the divers, and from where, by reaching out, he was able to grab the twisted lines. Frantically he struggled to untangle them, and at last he was successful. Then he guided the almost exhausted men onto the ladder and, hauling on their lifelines, helped them up, rung by rung, urging them on with threats and curses. But they could not hear him through their helmets, and, weighed down by their diving equipment and near to passing out for want of air, they climbed very slowly. There was still some way to go when Gammon saw the wave, arched like a cobra about to strike and foaming white at the top, racing at express speed toward them.

Desperately he strained on the ropes, willing the divers to safety, but at the same time certain that none of them would make it in time. Then, and it seemed to Gammon suddenly, they were at the top, and at that very moment the wave struck the pier to shatter the ladder and break over them in a tumult of spray and hissing brine.

Down in the South End, it seemed to Trevor Frowd that there were two explosions. First a dull rumble like thunder that shook the ground, and immediately afterwards a much louder, sharper bang. A blast of hot air made him stagger, and he saw windows in the houses around him disappear inward and the trees in the street bend against a sudden, violent wind. Then everything was quiet and seemingly normal once more. Puzzled, he hurried on again towards school.

A number of Halifax and Dartmouth residents later insisted that they also heard two explosions, and for many, the statement of the scientists—that the report was carried through both the earth and the air, and the earth, being a better conductor, brought the sound to them a little earlier than the air, the period between varying with the distance—fails even to this day to be a satisfactory explanation.

Of those near to the explosion centre who lived to speak of it, several said they heard nothing, but the majority were blinded temporarily by the flash, and all felt the power of the blast. The stories of amazing escapes were legion, and among them, that of Charles Mayers.

Mayers was third officer on the *Middleham Castle*. He had just returned on board, having been into town on business, when the *Mont Blanc* exploded. "There seemed to be no sound to it," he said some time afterwards, "but I was snatched up from the deck and tossed into the air."

As he was carried upward, he could not see anything, but he was spun wildly about and he was conscious of being in the midst of a vast cloud of wreckage. When at last he crashed to earth again and sat up, badly cut and bruised but miraculously alive, he found that he had been hurled to the top of Fort

Needham hill, half a mile away from his ship, and that he was naked save for his boots.

A peculiar feature of the blast was the many reports of people being stripped by it, but otherwise unharmed. An attractive young girl walking on Campbell Road was thrown to the sidewalk. She got to her feet again, frightened and in a daze of shock. No longer sure of where she was going, she wandered aimlessly for some time. Eventually a soldier stopped her and offered her his greatcoat, but she thought that he was trying to pick her up, and shook her head and tried to push past him. "I think you need it, miss, really I do," insisted the soldier. Puzzled, the girl looked down at herself and saw that all she had on were her corsets—even her stockings and shoes had been whipped away.

On the previous Tuesday, a poultry show had opened in the city market, and local fanciers had flocked to enter for it. The show had been scheduled to run for three days, but it closed abruptly on that Thursday morning when the airwave struck the building. Strangely, though, despite the fact that the market was extensively damaged, not one of the two thousand prize birds on display was injured in any way.

But elsewhere it was a very different story.

In Richmond and the North End, an area of roughly one square mile had been laid waste as completely as if a closely packed army of bulldozers had passed over it.

The dead lay thick among the ruins and on the streets, and for those trapped and buried under the wreckage, the only sound was of the flames as they roared nearer and nearer.

More than fifty horses died on the streets. Those that survived galloped away from the scene screaming with terror, many of them still harnessed to "slovens" or "teams" that pitched and leapt driverless behind their flying hooves.

Two hundred children, the matron, and every other member of the staff, died under the fallen roof and walls of the Protestant orphanage on Campbell Road. Those who were not killed outright were slowly burned to death.

Children of all ages were struck down across the city. They died in their homes, on the streets, and at their desks. One hundred of the pupils who had answered to the registers at Richmond School that morning were dead at six minutes past nine. At Roome Street, more than half the children perished. Fifty died in St. Joseph's School, and in other places, scores more were killed or injured. Three of the Richmond schools were totally destroyed, and throughout Halifax not one was habitable when the airwave had done its work.

As with the schools, so it was in offices, factories, and stores. Constant Upham, who sent in the alarm to the fire department, died with his customers in the shop on Campbell Road. The Canadian Government Railway lost sixty-one employees, among them Vincent Coleman, who was blasted to pieces at his telegraph key in the Richmond Yards. But not before his warning message had been heard in Rockingham and Truro, so that all incoming traffic was held up outside the danger zone. Few escaped with their lives who were on the dockside and the piers close to the explosion. The majority of them were either killed by the blast or swept away by the tidal wave and drowned, and of the seventy-five men in Hillis Foundry just north of Pier 6, only two survived.

Dozens of churches lay shattered or blasted away entirely, and in many instances whole parishes had been wiped out with them. Four hundred and four of the regular worshippers at the Anglican church of St. Mark's were killed, as were three hundred members of the congregation of the Roman Catholic chapel of St. Joseph's. In the roads around Grove Presbyterian and Kay Street Methodist churches, hundreds of their parishioners lay dead or dying.

In this moment of agony, a greater number had been killed

or injured in Halifax than ever were to be in any single air raid on London during the whole of World War Two.

Fire Chief Condon had been killed, and so had his deputy, William Brunt, their car a twisted mass of metal, upturned and on fire. Down by the pier for which she had been heading, the *Patricia* was a wreck, four of her crew of five dead around her; and everywhere flaming bonfires, fed by the heaped wreckage, raged out of control.

At 9:06 A.M. on Thursday, December 6, 1917, all normal life suddenly, terribly, and dramatically came to an end in Halifax. The town died. It would live again, but for a moment in its history, the city's heart stopped beating.

There was no gas or electricity. Little water flowed through the mains; the public transportation system had ceased to exist; the railway artery was severed; telephones were not working; and the telegraph lines, the only other means of communication with the outside world, were down.

For some time after the *Mont Blanc* blew up, the city was unnaturally quiet. Then it was bedlam. Everything that was ordered, familiar, and tranquil was gone, and horror, fear, and chaos reigned in their place. The elements of civilized society were broken down, and for many, all that remained was the jungle law of self-preservation. For others lay ahead the tasks of rescue and salvage, of counting the dead and estimating the damage, of rehabilitation and reconstruction.

CHAPTER SIX

THE WHITE ENSIGN

Rear Admiral Chambers, port convoy officer and senior British naval officer in Halifax, was at his home when a report of the collision and the fire on board *Mont Blanc* was telephoned to him. As one of the few men who knew the nature of the French freighter's cargo, he immediately realized the terrible danger to the city.

FROM: Rear Admiral B. M. Chambers, Port Convoy Officer and Senior Naval Officer (British), Halifax, N.S.
TO: The Secretary of the Admiralty (copy to C.-in-C.).
DATE: 6 December, 1917 No. Z/i
Submitted.

About 8.45 A.M. local time H.M.S. *Highflyer* reported *Imo* Belgian Relief Ship and *Mont Blanc,* French steamer to be in collision in Narrows. Shortly afterwards about 9 A.M. a second signal was received stating that the latter vessel was on fire.

A tremendous explosion took place at about 9.5 A.M. I immediately communicated with Vice Admiral E.R. Le Marchant who was present in the Port and on his arrival we went afloat in one of the Convoy Tugs, shortly after 9.30. As Vice Admiral Le Marchant had not hoisted his flag whilst in Port I took direction of affairs, though consulting him on important points, and I continued to do throughout the day.

I gave orders to the Commanding Officer *Changuinola* to land relief and stretcher parties taking the latter with me in the tug. I also signalled to *Highflyer* that all vessels able to do so should raise steam and be ready to leave wharves or get under way.

HMS *Changuinola,* a 5,978-ton vessel of the Elders & Fyffes fleet, had been commissioned for service as an armed merchant cruiser with the First Cruiser Squadron in December 1914. She had arrived in Halifax to form part of a convoy escort the evening before the disaster, and had anchored a little way upstream from the *Highflyer.* Although debris of all kinds fell around the merchant cruiser, she suffered only minor damage.

The damage to *Highflyer* was considerable, however, partly due to the blast and partly to falling wreckage. Her plating on the starboard side was split open, her wireless telegraphy cabin had been shattered, and the fore bridge, chart house, and captain's upper deck cabin and shelter smashed. Her standard and steering compass were badly damaged and useless, and after the explosion, the only boats on board that were seaworthy were one sailing pinnace, one galley, and a dinghy. On board the cruiser, three ratings were killed outright and fifty injured in varying degrees.

Leaving the *Changuinola,* accompanied by two surgeons and a number of stretcher bearers, Rear Admiral Chambers ordered the tug into the dockyard, where Vice Admiral Le Marchant disembarked to interview the Canadian senior naval officer, Captain Pasco. Chambers also put ashore here one of the surgeons and a party of bearers.

I next visited the *Highflyer* and obtained a report from Captain H. N. Garnett, R.N., and found that he had already landed a large party to assist on the Dartmouth side of harbour. He informed me that he feared Commander T. K. Triggs, R.N., and Lieutenant J. R. Ruffles, R.N.R., and the boat's crew who had been sent to the assistance of the burning vessel had perished.

From the *Highflyer* the scene was as follows. Two vessels *Middleham Castle* and *Picton*, were lying outside dry dock with their upper works in ruins. Between the *Middleham Castle* and the shore was a river collier *J. A. McKee*. I left the surgical party to attend to casualties on these vessels which all seemed much shaken by the explosion. A fire was now raging from the vicinity of the dry dock right up to Richmond and the top of the hill. Every building in the vicinity appeared to have been demolished. I left *Highflyer* with orders to try and haul off any vessels which appeared to be endangered by the fire and also giving warning to vessels at jettys to haul off wherever possible.

I then proceeded up through the Narrows to investigate the condition of Ships of Convoy in Bedford Basin. Passing through the Narrows it was necessary to exercise caution on account of the floating wreckage which almost blocked the way. The piers numbers 8 and 9 were almost unrecognisable. The steamer *Calonne* was alongside No. 9 with a heavy list and upper works demolished. A small tug, which afterwards proved to be the vessel chartered for use of Port Convoy Office, had been thrown completely over these wharves and was lying a complete wreck upon a pile of lumber 20 feet above the water. Upon the opposite side to S.E. of Brewery Wharf was the Belgian Relief Steamer *Imo* aground and upper works completely wrecked. About centre of Tuft's Cove was the wreck of the fine steamer *Curaca* which had been lying at Pier 8. She had apparently been carried across by the explosion and resulting wave. Her masts and funnel were broken off and stern bulged right in.

The weather was fortunately extremely fine and clear though cold and the wind, whilst variable, was mainly South, thus keeping the fire from spreading to the principal part of the city.

On entering Bedford Basin I closed the Guard Ship and was relieved to hear that the damage to ships of Convoy was slight. The Guard Ship, the nearest vessel, having sustained trivial damage.

In view of this I returned to the focus of the explosion which was in my opinion the Richmond Depot of the Intercolonial Railway. In passing I observed a person making signs for assistance and closing found as already stated that the wrecked tug *Hilford* was one of my own vessels which had been reported to me as safe. We landed and found confusion beyond description, the stacks of timber sheds and the railway track being inextricably mixed. In spite of these difficulties and with the very able assistance of Captain Turnbull, R.N.R. and the crew of the chartered tug *Maggie*, master Captain Gordon, I was able to rescue two of the crew of *Hilford*, one in a dying condition, besides two soldiers. The work involved in clearing a way for these badly injured men was great and I regret to state that we here found the body of my very able assistant Lieutenant Commander J. A. Murray, R.N.V.R., and although we were unable to extricate it from the immense quantity of debris which was pinning it down there could be no question either as to the identity or the impossibility of life existing. As the men rescued required urgent and immediate surgical attention I took them on board *Highflyer* and then proceeded to the Dockyard, feeling that, urgent as was the work of rescue, a report by myself after having become acquainted with the scope of the damage was of paramount importance.

It was not until the next day that a party of sailors from HM Escort Ship *Knight Templar*, working in the midst of a blinding snowstorm that had yet to develop when Chambers made this

HMCS *Niobe* in drydock, 1917. The Canadian navel vessel sustained damage in the explosion but was repaired and undertook further wartime missions.

report, finally managed, after hours of effort, to recover Murray's body from amid the wreckage on Pier 9.

By the time Chambers reached the dockyard again and boarded the *Niobe,* he had changed his mind about making a detailed report to the admiralty and the commander-in-chief North America and West Indies then and there. Instead he turned over the task of composing a signal, giving only a brief outline of the disaster to Captain Eldridge, the Canadian naval staff officer. Then he left the depot ship to confer with the captain superintendent of the dockyard.

Pasco had only just replaced the telephone receiver after talking to the transport office when the burning freighter against Pier 6 disintegrated. The bedroom window was blown in on him, and he was thrown to the floor with hundreds of tiny daggers of glass driven into his face, and with cuts on his head and hands. When he got up again, he was covered in blood and found he could hardly see.

His first thought was that the *Highflyer* had blown up, and he staggered downstairs and tried to leave the house by the front door. This proved to be impossible, however, as it was blocked with debris, so he went through to the kitchen and left by the back way.

With considerable difficulty Pasco made his way toward Pier 3. Despite his restricted vision he was conscious of the extensive damage around him and he could hear the cries of the wounded on all sides. When he reached the wharf he felt his legs begin to buckle under him, and he would have fallen had it not been for two men on a tug nearby who, seeing his condition, ran to him and took hold of his arms.

"Best come on board, sir, and we'll have a look-see at those cuts. They look very nasty."

The acting captain superintendent protested that he was all right and that he must be on his way, but the men would not listen. Between them, they half-carried him onto the deck of the tug and sat him down on a stool. And then one of them washed the wound on his head and bandaged it with a strip of linen torn from a sheet. Only when Pasco had promised to get proper medical attention for his wounds without delay would they let him go, and the captain, still unsteady on his feet, left the wharf and headed off in the direction of the dockyard administration block. He was still unaware of the cause of the explosion.

Pasco had not gone very far when he met Captain Hose, RCN, captain of patrols. Hose had been on board *Niobe* when the *Mont Blanc* had gone up, standing on the bridge with her first lieutenant. The two officers had witnessed the monstrous eruption and had been sent reeling by the blast that levelled the row of wooden offices on deck and crumpled two funnels. But they had not been injured, and they had reached the shelter of the conning tower before hundredweights of debris crashed onto the deck and the tidal wave treated the cruiser's eleven thousand tons with the contemptuous nonchalance of a pond ripple bobbing an empty bottle. The ship had been thrust upward, hung for a moment poised, and then lurched down with rolls from port to starboard that parted her from her after moorings.

As soon as he could, Hose had left the *Niobe* to be on hand in the dockyard. When he met Pasco, he told him about the *Mont Blanc* and then suggested that they both station themselves in front of the captain superintendent's house, this being a central position to which all reports of damage and casualties could be relayed to them.

The Canadian senior naval officer agreed, and for some time the two men worked together, sifting the information that came in and directing rescue operations. By eleven o'clock, though, Pasco was in considerable pain and he was steadily losing what little sight he had, and he was reluctantly forced to hand over his duties and full responsibility to his deputy.

So it was with Captain Hose that Chambers had his meeting. The admiral requested that Hose have the Narrows sounded as quickly as possible to establish whether there were any obstructions to navigation, and suggested that, in the meantime, all shipping be prohibited from entering or leaving the harbour. After also discussing with him the question of patrols and piquets and, having received Hose's authorization as Canadian senior naval officer—now that Pasco had withdrawn from duty—to speak for him when interviewing the general officer commanding of Halifax, Chambers left the dockyard and boarded the convoy vice admiral's flagship, *Knight Templar.* Later that afternoon he was to receive a report from Hose that the channel was clear.

By noon the fire had reached the dry dock close to the steamer *Picton,* moored alongside the Sugar Refinery wharf.

The *Picton,* which had fouled a rock when entering harbour and had fractured her propeller and rudder, was carrying a cargo of loaded shells. The stevedores had already started unloading her so that she could be repaired when the explosion occurred. The blast killed or severely injured most of those men on board who were exposed, and the vessel was extremely badly damaged.

With the nearness of the flames around the dry dock, the merchant ship was towed away from the wharf by naval tugs and anchored in midstream. But this was not to be the end of the *Picton*'s part in the affair, for she was destined to become the centre of a fierce controversy.

When he left *Knight Templar,* Chambers went into the city for a meeting with the Canadian major general commanding the Halifax military district.

About 3 p.m. I met General Benson and was able to acquaint him with the general situation from the naval point of view. He gave me a very courteous reception and asked me to accompany him to a meeting convened by the Lieutenant Governor at the Town Hall. This I did.

On leaving the Town Hall I returned to my office where I found Vice Admiral Le Marchant and Captain H. N. Garnett, R.N., of the *Highflyer.* I discussed the situation with them, particularly with regard to the fact that certain of the crew of the two ships which collided were now on board H.M.S. *Highflyer* and as to the question of their presence at any inquiry which might take place. We decided to consult the Lieutenant Governor on this point.

When I was about to leave to see the Lieutenant Governor, Captain Powers-Symington, U.S.S. *Tacoma* and Commander Moses, U.S.S. *Von Steuben,* arrived to offer any help in their power and to report the arrival of their ships. I took these officers to the headquarters of the General Officer Commanding where they were welcomed and arrangements made to utilise the services offered. I then went to Government House where the Lieutenant Governor favourably received my suggestions re. crews of *Imo* and *Mont Blanc.*

Captain Hines, Liaison Officer, U.S.N., at this Port, had very promptly placed at the disposal of the naval authorities the U.S. vessel *Old Colony* for service as extempore hospital ship and I therefore requested that any medical help which the *Tacoma* and *Von Steuben* could afford might be sent to this ship where I was informed such help was urgently needed.

In conclusion no description of mine can adequately picture the devastation which has befallen this city. For miles every window has been reduced to fragments and in parts far from the explosion houses have collapsed. My office has been isolated and windows broken and the office generally disorganised.

B. M. CHAMBERS,
Rear Admiral,
Senior Naval Officer.

On December 7 and 8, Captain H. N. Garnett, HMS *Highflyer;* Captain J. Willcox, HMS *Changuinola;* and the other naval officers concerned with the rescue operations made their reports.

Garnett's, addressed to Rear Admiral Chambers, began with an outline of the collision and explosion as seen from *Highflyer,* detailed the dispatch of Commander Triggs and his party in the whaler, and then, after listing the damage to his ship, dealt with the situation in the harbour and the steps the captain had taken in organizing relief.

The pinnace was used for rescuing injured from other ships, persons from vessels on fire and particularly in communicating with S.S. *Picton* which was found to contain ammunition. As the fire ashore was rapidly approaching that ship every effort was made to attract the attention of tugs to endeavour to remove her and she was eventually hauled off.

The galley of *Highflyer* was also employed in rescuing injured men from various vessels and communicating with the shore. The dinghy, manned by a volunteer crew with *Highflyer's* schoolmaster, William T. Shapland, in charge, went away to search in the vicinity where the whaler was last seen. The dinghy was away for several hours in all and worked very well in a temperature below freezing point.

They were eager to continue with their work but, as I considered that it was then hopeless, she was subsequently used for communication with the shore.

During their first search, the crew of *Highflyer's* dinghy spotted Able Seaman Murphy, semi-conscious in the water and supported by two oars. He was immediately taken back to the ship, but died within a few minutes of arrival. It was on the dinghy's second trip that Becker was found. He had just managed to make it to the shore before he passed out. An engine driver discovered him, dragged him from the water, and carried him up to the railway line above, where he revived him in the warmth from an open engine furnace. Still very shaky, Becker was rowed to the *Highflyer* and put into sick bay, where eventually he recovered.

During the forenoon I noticed that the tug *Musquash,* secured alongside the S.S. *Middleham Castle,* was on fire and that the fire was increasing. She had a gun and ammunition on board and there appeared to be a danger of her getting adrift and drifting down onto the *Picton.* I hailed a private tug and asked her to take her away but they were unwilling to board the *Musquash* to get her in tow. I got her alongside *Highflyer* and two of the ship's company, Leading Seaman Thomas N. Davis and Able Seaman

Robert Stones, volunteered to go on board the burning *Musquash*. They got into the private tug which approached the *Musquash* which, by this time, had actually broken adrift and was nearing the *Picton* and these two men jumped aboard, secured a line to her stern and she was towed to midstream. Here the tow line parted and the *Musquash* drifted free again.

Commander Hollaway, in the pumping vessel *Lee*, then arrived and the two men passed another line from the *Musquash* to the *Lee*. They then both went forward to the burning part and succeeded in getting the ammunition, which by this time was badly scorched, and pulled it away from the flames and threw it overboard. They then broke open the door of the galley which was on fire inside to enable the *Lee* to play her hoses into it. They repeated the same thing with the cabin. By their work Commander Hollaway was able to subdue the fire and save the tug. The *Lee* did magnificent work, not only here but in going from vessel to vessel attacking fires.

The party of engine-room ratings who had landed under Engineer Commander John W. Hopkyns and Acting Warrant Mechanician Hicks—some fifty strong—carried out most valuable rescue work on the Dartmouth shore, remaining there for six hours only being recalled because it was considered advisable to have steam on the main engines and unmoor the ship. One party, after having taken injured people from buildings, took them to hospital; others were employed in collecting beds and bedding from the surrounding houses and taking patients to the hospital. The engineroom artificers collected injured children, organised and carried out first aid and bandaging work at a school. Engineer Commander Hopkyns with Warrant Mechanician Hicks and the remainder of the stokers went from house to house rescuing and collecting a large number of injured. Hopkyns also collected and brought on board twenty-eight of the crew of the *Mont Blanc*.

The crew members of the *Mont Blanc* were wandering around the countryside in a dazed and aimless condition. They were very difficult to control and had to be handled with firmness.

By the end of the day, the *Highflyer* had also taken on board a number of survivors and injured from the *Imo*. On Rear Admiral Chambers's instructions, and with the approval of the lieutenant governor, these men and the men from the *Mont Blanc* were held on board, pending an inquiry into the collision.

In addition to the injured of *Highflyer*, a good many seriously injured men were brought on board from various vessels, and stretcher and first aid parties were organised and worked under Fleet Surgeon John Macdonald throughout the day and the following night. Fleet Surgeon worked continuously for many hours operating and patching. Surgeon Jennings assisted him in this work up to 3.0 P.M. when, on landing in the Dockyard, I found many serious cases were being landed by boats and carried on board the U.S.S. *Old Colony* but that there were on board no doctors or nurses. Three or four of these cases died while they were still on the jetty so I sent for Surgeon Jennings and two naval nurses and these three started and carried on most valuable work in that vessel.

Early in the forenoon I gave orders for the marine detachments from *Highflyer* and *Changuinola*, under Lieutenant Simonds, R.M.L.I., to be landed and round up all naval ratings in the town and return them to the Dockyard and their vessels. They were also to patrol the town continuously and assist the military in preserving order, dealing specially with naval ratings. These orders were quickly carried out and the marine detachments remained on shore until 7.30 P.M. when the patrolling of the town was taken over by United States seamen from U.S.S. *Tacoma* and U.S.S. *Von Steuben*.

Lieutenant Commander J. J. Brewer, R.N., who took over as Executive Officer of H.M.S. *Highflyer* when Triggs went away with the whaler served with great ability.

H. N. GARNETT,
Captain.

FROM: Captain H. J. L. W. K. Willcox, R.N., H.M.S. *Changuinola.*
TO: Rear Admiral B. M. Chambers, Senior Naval Officer (British), Halifax.
DATE: 7 December, 1917.

Upon explosion I immediately ordered a strong landing party with ten officers under Acting Lieutenant Commander F. H. D. Clarke, R.N.R., to land at once, render aid and report situation. To send one party to magazine to ascertain that all precautions had been taken there and render assistance generally. The landing party went ashore astern of *Niobe*. Surgeon Brown with No. 1 stretcher party and Surgeon Blackburn with No. 2 stretcher party and first aid chest were landed in Rear Admiral Chambers' steamboat at 9.35 A.M.

Lieutenant E. B. Thompson, R.N.R., and Midshipman Cluff, R.N.R., entered the magazine and when the malicious report that the magazine was on fire spread immediately took steps to allay and disprove the report. I consider many lives were lost and endangered owing to this alarm as several thinly clad women and children, also injured, fled into Point Pleasant Park and hid in the bushes.

Steam was ordered on main engines and ship was unmoored and ready to shift berth if required at 11.30 A.M. with towing hawsers ready. This was reported to *Niobe* for transmission to Rear Admiral Chambers.

Eleven available marines were landed at 1.0 P.M. to patrol streets, etc. under Captain of Marines of Highflyer.

Remains of the Hillis Foundry (at left). Only two of the seventy-five employees survived the destruction. President Frank Hillis also perished in the blast, and the Campbell Road foundry was never rebuilt.

The landing party under Acting Lieutenant Commander Clarke, R.N.R., returned at 3.10 P.M.

J. WILLCOX,
Captain.

FROM: Acting Lieutenant Commander Francis H. Drake-Clarke.
TO: Commanding Officer H.M.S. *Changuinola.*
DATE: 7 December, 1917.

On landing I made for the conflagration by the shortest route detailing on the way Lieutenant E. B. Thompson, R.N.R. and one company of men to assist at the magazine. I worked my remaining three companies round the fire by the waterfront and split them up into sections with orders to work independently overhauling the ruins and pulling out the wounded, leaving only the dead.

At first when there was a practicable track leading back to the city I ordered all the wounded and walking cases to be taken back to the city side of the fire, but as we advanced over the fire this was not possible so I ordered all cases to be taken down to the waterfront from whence we conveyed them in our cutters, greatly assisted by tugboat *Togo* and some drifters which were acquired by the initiative of Lieutenants Richard Peat, R.N.R. and Herbert Percival, R.N.R. and proved of inestimable value in taking large numbers of very bad cases up to the clearing station astern of *Niobe*.

The work was of very severe nature owing to the falling timbers, heat and smoke and the choked up nature of all the ground, but all my officers and men worked like Trojans until we had cleared the hillside of all with life in them who could be got at, many of these died in transit and many more lived.

A number of soldiers appeared about two hours after we had commenced and being without officers or any organisation I took command of as many as I could get and turned them to account as stretcher parties.

Much harm was caused by foolish people spreading alarm amongst the civilians that the magazine was on fire and so drawing them into the bush and frightening still more the injured. Lieutenant E. B. Thompson brought back many other people to be attended to by means of a commandeered wagon.

About 2.30 P.M. I collected most of my men, except the doctor's party and returned on board.

FRANCIS H. DRAKE-CLARKE,
Act. Lieutenant Commander, R.N.R

The rumour that the magazine was on fire and that a second explosion was imminent spread rapidly, and resulted in a further wave of terror and panic throughout the city. The story was, however, completely untrue. The facts were that any danger was averted by the prompt action of the soldiers of the 72nd Ottawa Battalion guarding the magazine, under the command of

Lieutenant Olmstead, working alongside companies of sailors from the ships in the harbour. Much of the ammunition in store was carried away and stacked in a place of safety, and as an extra precaution, the remainder, together with the interior of the magazine, was thoroughly soaked with water.

FROM: Lieutenant Sidney W. Baker, R.N.R.
TO: Commanding Officer, H.M.S. *Changuinola.*
DATE: 7 December, 1917.

At 9.30 A.M. on the 6 December, I landed in charge of my division under Lieutenant Commander F. H. D. Clarke, R.N.R. On landing I received orders to employ my division in rescue work which comprised clearing debris and extracting bodies from ruins. Many cases were badly injured and survived minutes only. With improvised stretchers and any assistance we carried cases to what remained of a stone jetty. I obtained two tugs from *Niobe, C.D.14* and *Togo,* and proceeded to embark the injured. Thirty cases were conveyed in this manner to hospital ship *Old Colony.*

The whole of the rescue work was made difficult owing to flames, smoke and falling timbers. My party was very much separated during the carrying process and rescue work, but the whole of my division worked splendidly.

At 2.45 all possible rescue work had ceased in the vicinity of the fire and I returned to jetty alongside *Niobe.* At 3 p.m. we returned to ship under Lieutenant Commander Clarke.

S. W. BAKER,
Lieutenant, R.N.R.

When he returned to the *Changuinola,* Baker confided to his friend Lieutenant Victor Magnus, RNVR, that the morning's work had been the most harrowing experience of his life. Rescue among the wreckage of the houses was extremely difficult, and speed was essential because of the rapid spread of the fire. In many cases, whole families had to be left where they were to burn to death because others could be got at more easily and quickly. Baker was sickened at having to abandon them, but he had no alternative if he were to save anyone at all.

"My one regret was that I did not have my revolver with me," he told Magnus. "At least then I could have spared them further pain and suffering."

FROM : Lieutenant Herbert Percival, R.N.R.
TO: Commanding Officer, H.M.S. *Changuinola*.
DATE : 7 December, 1917.

At 9.30 A.M. on the 6 December, I landed with the foretop division under command of Lieutenant Commander Clarke, R.N.R. Arriving at the vicinity where the explosion had occurred Clarke gave orders for us to work independently by divisions to assist wounded to a place of safety and search the ruins for survivors. I worked along the railway track and soon arrived at the centre of the fire. Many wounded were carried to a place of safety and my division was very quickly exhausted. I utilised the services of any soldiers or civilians I could see but unfortunately the demand exceeded the supply.

Many badly injured were pulled from under houses which had collapsed and I am sorry to say a few had to be abandoned as the houses crashed down in flames. There were no available means of extinguishing the fire.

At about 11 A.M., the railway track, which had been the only safe means of communication, became impassable owing to fire. A large number of injured had been collected and carried down to the waterfront.

I worked outside the fire along the waterfront, picked up a few seamen en route, manned four cutters and brought them round to where the wounded had been collected and subsequently loaded them several times and transported the injured to the Dockyard jetty.

Motor-cars were then commandeered and the wounded sent to hospital. In the meantime the military had arrived on the scene.

About 2.30 P.M. all houses which were not burning badly had been searched and as no more wounded were to be found I joined up with Lieutenant Commander Clarke and returned on board.

H. PERCIVAL,
Lieutenant, R.N.R.

FROM: Lieutenant Ernest Bass Thompson, R.N.R.
TO: Commanding Officer, H.M.S. *Changuinola.*
DATE: 7 December, 1917.

I was in charge of the quarter deck division, this being one of four divisions landed under command of Lieutenant Commander F. H. D. Clarke, R.N.R. On landing I was detailed to proceed with my division to assist a military officer at the magazine, to see what damage was done inside. While I was there a report outside was circulated that the magazine was on fire and this scattered all my party outside clearing away wreckage as they were ordered to get down to the waterfront.

Midshipman Arthur W. Cluff, R.N.R., was on top of the magazine with the military officer. When I came out I found some of the men picking up wounded people on the railway line and we got them conveyed to hospital in a cart. I then got together two or three sailors from various ships and commenced getting the wounded out of the burning houses and carrying them to the end of the street where motors picked them up eventually and took them to hospital. Later in the morning I came across Lieutenant Commander F. H. D. Clarke, Midshipman Restell-Little and Midshipman Arthur W. Cluff, R.N.R., and we all continued searching for living people among the ruins and getting them carried to a place of safety.

During these operations Midshipman Arthur W. Cluff, R.N.R. and myself got separated from Clarke and Restell-Little. We continued getting bodies out of houses, attending the wounded we came across and leaving the dead to be picked up later on.

Midshipman Cluff worked remarkably well and showed great self-control and coolness in dealing with what really were most horrible cases.

We then fell in with some American sailors and continued to search house after house. At three o'clock all the houses in the district we were working in had been searched and we then made our way down to the waterfront. Here we met four or five men from the *Changuinola* and I procured a boat from a ship alongside and came off to *Changuinola* bringing the men with me. I reported on board at 3.30 P.M.

E. B. THOMPSON,
Lieutenant, R.N.R.

For weeks before the explosion, young Midshipman Cluff, who worked so well alongside Lieutenant Thompson, had spent much of his off-duty time rehearsing for *Changuinola's* Christmas pantomime. Because of his good looks, the boy was chosen from an all-ranks cast to play "Clinkeremma," the female lead. Despite considerable ragging from the other midshipmen on board, Cluff threw himself wholeheartedly into the part and enjoyed the somewhat chaotic rehearsals immensely.

By December 6 the programmes for the pantomime had been printed:

THE TENTH CRUISER SQUADRON EMPIRES UNLIMITED
Theatre Royal, "Changuinola"
R. Houghton (by arrangement with Crosse & Blackwells, Swan & Edgars, and the Y.W. (or M.) C.A. produces and presents the event of the 15th Century entitled:
"CLINKEREMMA"
being an attempt at Pantomime reconstructed on the remains of one, Cinderalla, Guardian of Ashes (always with the usual apologies).
This Pantomime has been passed by the Board of Censors, Minister of Munitions, Horatio B....y, and will probably be passed by every other person immediately after witnessing the Performance.

After the disaster, though, the men of *Changuinola* were too much affected by the awful scenes ashore to find any enjoyment in going on with the show, and it was cancelled.

FROM: Lieutenant A. Webster, R.N.R., H.M.S. *Knight Templar.*
TO: Rear Admiral B. M. Chambers, Senior Naval Officer (British), Halifax.
DATE: 7 December, 1917.

A landing party from H.M. Escort Ship *Knight Templar* under the command of Lieutenant A. S. M. Nicholls, R.N.R., proceeded to the Dockyard, reported to the Captain Superintendent, and proceeded to search buildings for dead and wounded. The wounded were taken by motor-car to Y.M.C.A. Hall which had been improvised as a hospital and here Surgeon Probationer Archibald Glen Duncan, R.N.V.R., took charge single-handed and, assisted by ladies, rendered excellent service.

The party then proceeded to the military magazine with buckets of water to prevent fires, no hydrants being in the vicinity. The military magazine was isolated as far as possible of all woodwork and the party then proceeded to extinguish a fire at the northern end of the Barracks.

After this they assisted the City Fire Brigade until 2.30 p.m. when the officer in charge of the Brigade stated that as far as this area was concerned he was satisfied that the situation was in hand. The party then returned to the Dockyard and then to their ship. .

A. WEBSTER.
Lieutenant, R.N.R.
Commanding Officer.

Among the reports to Captain Willcox of HMS *Changuinola* was that of surgeon Horace G. Brown, RN, the ship's senior medical officer.

Together with surgeon W. H. Blackburn, he was taken off in Rear Admiral Chambers's tug at 9:30 A.M. on the 6th and put in charge of the stretcher party that was landed astern of the *Niobe*.

Acting on the orders of Vice Admiral Le Marchant, Brown and his men proceeded to search the dockyard for wounded, going as far north from their point of landing as the fire would permit.

I first of all found two ratings who were very seriously wounded; they were rendered first aid and dispatched, one in the ship's stretcher and the other on an improvised stretcher to the nearest hospital, in charge of Sick Berth Attendant Charles A. Fleet. I then proceeded alone to render first aid to any wounded I could find in the neighbouring houses which were practically all demolished. In the ruined basement of one of these I found Staff Surgeon Rousseau, R.C.N. who had been severely wounded but who had carried on with his work until he collapsed from loss of blood. I rendered him first aid and later in the day had him transferred to the hospital ship *Old Colony*.

I then proceeded on board vessels lying alongside the wharf

and rendered first aid to those who had been injured thereon or who had been removed there, which number included naval ratings and civilians, the majority of the latter being women and children. On one of these vessels I rendered first aid to Captain F. C. C. Pasco, R.N. who was suffering from severe lacerations of the face.

Later on I superintended the removal of the dead and wounded to the hospital ship *Old Colony* and rendered first aid on board that ship until 6 P.M. I then transferred the two most seriously wounded in an ambulance from that ship to Camp Hill Hospital. At this hospital I placed myself at the disposal of Major Morris who was in command and worked there operating and dressing until midnight. I returned on board my ship at 2 A.M. on the 7th inst.

In accordance with instructions received from Major Morris I returned to Camp Hill Hospital after breakfast, 6 A.M. on the 7th inst. and worked there until the evening when I proceeded to the hospital ship *Old Colony* to render any further assistance that might be necessary. Owing to the blizzard which was raging I was unable to return on board my ship and so slept on the hospital ship where I received the greatest kindness and hospitality. I returned to my ship at 9 A.M. on the 8th inst. On the afternoon of this day I visited the ships *Margaret* and *Hochelaga* where I dressed those cases which were still remaining on board and gave notice that a surgeon would be available at any hour on board my ship if his services were required.

During the whole of the time I was attending the wounded all the instruments and dressings which were on my ship were utilised as the occasion demanded, the supply of surgical instruments, dressings and anaesthetics ashore (other than those from H.M. ships) being hopelessly inadequate.

Special mention must be made of valuable aid rendered to the wounded by Sick Berth Attendant Charles A. Fleet and Leading Telegraphist Richard B. Askins who were working at times in positions of great danger to themselves. Further mention must be made of Mrs. Shepherd, a nurse, 276 Robie Street, Halifax, who came to the Dockyard with a copious supply of first aid dressings and who, assisted by Able Seaman Alfred J. Smoker, *Changuinola*, worked indefatigably amongst the wounded until 4 P.M. She and Smoker then proceeded to Camp Hill Hospital where Mrs. Shepherd continued to work until 10 P.M. when she approached beds to find her mother and sister who had been removed there, both seriously wounded and dying.

Smoker continued to work at Camp Hill Hospital throughout the night rendering valuable assistance.

H. G. BROWN

Ty. Surgeon, R.N.

The blizzard referred to in the reports began as a gentle flurry very early on the morning of the 7th. Almost immediately following the explosion, the temperature had dropped hour by hour, and at 10:00 A.M. on Friday, the snow, driven by a fierce wind, had reduced visibility to not more than two yards and was forming deep drifts, making the work of rescue parties throughout the city impossible.

The storm attained its maximum height during the night of the 7th to the 8th, and several ships dragged their anchors in what was one of the most severe gales Halifax had known for many years. By midday on Saturday, however, the weather was much improved; it had stopped snowing and the wind had fallen away to a breeze. But within hours conditions changed again and heavy rain set in, whipped to a driving torrent by a strong southerly gale, and soon the streets were knee to waist-deep in liquid slush which, once this storm had passed and the temperature fell again, froze solid.

It was almost as if Fate, unconvinced that the exploding chemicals in the hold of the *Mont Blanc* had struck a death blow to Halifax, was now calling upon Nature to administer the *coup de grace*.

CHAPTER SEVEN
"THE END OF THE WHOLE BLOODY WORLD"

When Mrs. Clark emerged again from her burning home, her face was blackened by the smoke and her clothes and hair were scorched and singed. But she had found the precious teapot, and she carried it out, protected under her apron.

By now fires raged on all sides, and showers of sparks cascaded onto the lawn around the two women and the injured William Fowlie. It was obvious to all three that it would not be safe for them to remain there much longer. Evacuation, though, presented a problem. The pain in Fowlie's chest and legs still made it impossible for him to stand, and his landlady and her daughter were not strong enough to carry him.

"Don't you fret now, I'll get some help," Mrs. Clark, calm and practical once more, assured the young man. "Just you rest there," she said and then she hurried away out of sight.

Two men who Fowlie knew vaguely as neighbours were with her when she returned. They had clearly been badly shaken themselves, but both were anxious to help. Without hesitating, they tore away some boards from the garden fence and, laying the improvised stretcher on the ground, lifted Fowlie onto it.

Then they carried him around by the side of the house and out into the street.

Here, having ensured his safety, Mrs. Clark and her daughter said goodbye, explaining that they intended to stay and give what assistance they could. Fowlie took his leave of them, begging them to take care and then his bearers started off down the road with him.

Russell Street no longer existed. Nearly every house on it had crumpled under the blast into a pile of shattered wreckage. Even the few that had one or two walls still standing were otherwise totally demolished, and many were blazing. Here and there people were frantically searching among the ruins or vainly trying to extinguish the blaze, and Fowlie saw the lifeless body of an elderly woman lying face downward across a beam.

The roadway had disappeared entirely beneath the debris, so that the two men carrying the stretcher, stumbling and lurching over rubble, had great difficulty in making their way down to the main road above the waterfront.

Lockman Street was also littered with wreckage, but here the going was a little easier, and they managed to get Fowlie over to the low wall that ran along by the sidewalk and which overlooked the destruction around the dry dock. They laid the wooden stretcher onto the parapet, and having made sure it was secure, one of the men said, "There'll be people along soon I guess. They'll see you. We've got to get back to our families, you understand?"

Fowlie nodded and thanked them for their help, and then they ran back in the direction from which they had come.

For some time the young Englishman lay there without seeing anyone. He could hear the noise of the fires that burned on the piers and among the demolished acres of what had once been Richmond, and the anguished cries of survivors calling out to

The Richmond area of Halifax's North End lay in ruins following the explosion.

others trapped beneath fallen roofs and walls. But as yet there was no sign of any organized relief.

In a little while, though, scores of men and women who had been at work or shopping downtown at the time of the explosion came hurrying along the street. Their faces were white and drawn, and their eyes searched desperately for any familiar landmark that would tell them they were close to the street on which they lived, where, an hour or so earlier, they had left their families. Stunned by the terrible sight and sick with horror and anxiety, none of them even noticed Fowlie lying on the parapet.

As long as he did not try to move his pain was not very great but, uncovered and wearing only a suit, he shivered violently in the bitter cold. Suddenly he heard the sound of excited shouting and a woman scream in terror. He lifted his head a little from the boards in an attempt to see what was going on. People were running everywhere. They poured down over the wreckage on the hillside, emerging through the smoke in a confused, broken wave. Some tripped and fell, and were kicked and trodden on by those behind. Others thrust and barged their way savagely into the lead.

When the stampeding herd of humanity reached Lockman Street, it did not turn toward the city, but swept away in the direction of the open ground around Bedford Basin, a straggling terrified mob.

As people ran past him, Fowlie called out and asked what was happening, but nobody seemed to hear him, for he got no answer. In a matter of seconds the street was empty; there was not a living creature to be seen; everyone had fled and he was alone. Up on the hill, the isolated fires joined one with another and massed into a single furious blaze that spread rapidly to engulf many of the forsaken injured.

Just how long he lay on the wall William Fowlie never knew, for after witnessing the unexplained panic, he lost all track of time and, numbed by the cold, he seemed to drift in and out of consciousness, half-fainting, half asleep.

He was dimly aware that someone was talking close at hand, and he opened his eyes to find a sailor bending over him. "Here's one that's alive," the man called over his shoulder. "Come and get hold of the other end." Another sailor came into Fowlie's vision, and gave him the thumbs up sign. "You'll be all right now, mate. The navy's here," he said.

Between them, the two men carried the makeshift stretcher over to a horse-drawn cart and lifted it into it. There were already a number of injured on board, some lying on the floor, some sitting propped against the sides.

When they had him stowed away, the first sailor got into the driver's seat and took the reins, and his companion, a much older man, clambered up onto the tailboard and sat alongside Fowlie, whom he covered with his overcoat. As the cart rattled and bumped over heaps of debris, the sailor took out a bag of tobacco and some papers and expertly rolled a cigarette.

"Looks like the end of the whole bloody world, don't it?" he said, indicating the desolation around them with a movement of his head. "Never think they'd be able to pack enough explosives into one little ship to do all that, would you?" Then, finding that Fowlie did not know what had happened, he told him about the *Mont Blanc,* and explained that he and his friend were part of one of the rescue parties. Somehow they had got separated from the rest and had decided to work independently.

"When we came across the fellow who had this cart we asked him to let us have it, but he wasn't too keen. So I had to hit him, and then we commandeered it, so to speak. Just as well we did, I reckon, we're going to need it. Looks like it's going to be a busy day." Then, tipping his cap forward over his eyes, he settled back to enjoy his smoke.

By the time Fowlie was picked up, service relief parties and civilian rescuers had begun to requisition vehicles of all kinds in which to transport the dead and the injured, to supplement those already volunteered by citizens. As the day went on they were to acquire many more. In the majority of cases, those cars or wagons that were commandeered were handed over willingly, but in some instances owners at first refused point-blank and had either to be persuaded or forced into complying. Faced with a situation such as this, the soldiers and sailors seldom wasted time with talk.

A detail of the 63rd Halifax Rifles came across a man heading away from the disaster area in his car. They stopped him and asked him to place the vehicle at their disposal, but his answer was, "Oh! I'd like to help, believe me, but this is a new car and the last thing I want is to get blood all over the seats."

The soldiers were not in the mood to argue. Hauling the struggling, squealing man from his seat, they tossed him into the gutter and then drove off in the direction of Richmond.

The sailors with the delivery cart took Fowlie and the other injured to Victoria General Hospital, to find it already filled to overflowing. Every available bed was occupied, and casualties were being laid in the hall and corridors and even on the floor between the beds in the wards.

Throughout the city, every hospital, both military and civil, was in a similar position. Even when the YMCA, YWCA, church halls, cinemas, theatres, and the Academy of Music, together with other buildings, had been turned into relief and first aid centres, it was still not possible to give attention to all the wounded.

Fowlie was taken into the Victoria General Hospital and transferred to a hospital stretcher, which was set down in a corner of the entrance hall. From his position, he was to see, throughout the day, an endless procession of stretchers, real and improvised, being carried up the winding staircase, the hospital elevator having been put out of action by the failure of the electricity supply.

Lack of power was not the only problem for the medical staff. The superintendent was out of town, and Dr. C. E. Puttner, who had taken charge following the explosion, quite early on collapsed with a heart attack and for some time became a patient himself. There was no one, therefore, to coordinate the vast amount of work, and there was little organization among the staff. By noon, a further crisis arose when it became obvious to everyone that the limited reserves of drugs and anesthetics in the hospital would soon be exhausted.

As with everywhere else, a considerable number of the cases admitted to the Victoria General were people who had been blinded or had sustained optic injuries as a result of the flying particles of glass, and one of the principal operations that the surgeons were called upon to perform was the removal of eyes embedded with splinters.

Such was the confusion, and so great the number of obviously badly injured admitted, that it was not until the following day that a doctor was able to spare any time for Fowlie. His diagnosis, after a hasty examination, was that the young man was suffering from a fractured rib cage with possible complications, and he had him transferred to a bed in one of the wards.

On Saturday his condition had worsened, and on the afternoon of that day he was moved by ambulance to the USS *Old Colony,* which was being used as a hospital ship and to which many of the terribly injured had been carried.

Aboard this old vessel that looked for all the world like one of the Mississippi showboats, the surgeons from the American cruisers *Tacoma* and *Von Steuben* were working round the clock operating and dressing wounds, with the assistance of women volunteers from the city.

By Tuesday the suspected complications to Fowlie's injuries had set in, and he went down with pleurisy quickly followed by pneumonia, no doubt due to his long exposure to the bitter cold during the time he had lain on the parapet. For many days he was on the danger list, but then, slowly, he began to respond to treatment, and a day or two before Christmas, his condition having greatly improved, he was taken ashore by stretcher and placed in the care of friends, one of whom was a registered nurse, and he stayed with them until he had fully recovered.

With the cries of those who lay wounded and dying in the cotton factory still ringing in her ears, Lillian Atkins ran until she was exhausted, and then, gasping for breath, she fell back for support against a wall. She wanted so much to cry but somehow the tears would not come, and overwhelmed by a feeling of utter weariness and helplessness, she sat down. She did not know what had happened or what would become of her; she knew only that she was alive.

She sat on the sidewalk for some time, unaware of very much around her, until two young soldiers from Wellington Barracks came over and asked if they could help.

Lillian looked up. "I want to go home," she said simply.

The soldiers said they would take her there and she gave them the address of the boarding house in King's Place.

As they made their way carefully over the thick carpet of wreckage that was all around them, and which had covered the streets so as to make it impossible to distinguish them, one of the men struggled out of his greatcoat and insisted that the shivering girl put it on.

It was possible to see for some considerable distance over the desolated and flattened area and, to Lillian's surprise, there was not another living person in sight. Bodies, lying in hideous, contorted attitudes, some of them terribly mutilated, were scattered everywhere. Now and then a muffled and frantic call for help or the shrill scream of a child in pain could be heard coming from somewhere beneath the debris. But there seemed to be no one to answer them; no one to tear away the beams under which they were pinned.

From behind one of the few walls that were still standing, a horse suddenly appeared, harnessed to a small cart. The cart was piled with corpses, stacked like cords of wood, and as it bucketed over the uneven ground behind the now ambling, now scavenging, unattended animal, some of them were dislodged and either fell off, or slipped to the sides, like discarded puppets, to trail an arm or a leg.

At last the girl and her two companions reached what, between them, they worked out must be King's Place, but they found that the boarding house was no longer standing. Where it had once been, a huge bonfire now shot flames high into the air.

Lillian turned away, stunned, unable to think of what she would do or where she would go now. Her one thought was of her landlady and the other members of the family who had taken her in and treated her so well, and in her mind she saw again the wooden cart with its jolting load of death. When the soldiers suggested that they find a doctor to attend to the cuts on her face and arms, she said nothing and let them lead her away.

They went down into the city, and on the way a fire engine passed them, and then they saw more and more people and they were glad, for they had thought at first that they must be the only survivors. For a long time they walked the streets, going from one surgery to another but without success. Every available doctor had been called to the hospitals and the first aid stations had not yet been set up. So, at last, they wearily wandered back in the direction of Richmond, past trams that had been hurled from the tracks, and around and over vast masses of rubble.

On Gottingen Street, Lillian said that she could not walk any further and, as it was nearby, the soldiers took her into Wellington Barracks. There were few people about and no one on the gate to stop them, so they took her into their quarters, where all the glass had been blown from the windows and the door was off its hinges, and where, in places, the roof had caved in. Here the soldiers told her to rest, and then they went away. Lillian unrolled the palliasse on one of the beds and sank down onto it gratefully. Soon she was asleep.

Wellington Barracks had been badly hit by the blast, and in a letter to his father written the day after the explosion, Paymaster Captain Simpson describes the scene.

Halifax, N.S., 7 December, 1917

Dear Dad,

I presume that by the time you receive this you will have read in the papers of the terrible disaster here, but possibly an account of the affair, as I have been able to gather it, will be of interest to you.

Our offices had been moved down to Wellington Barracks on Tuesday. I got in from St John on Wednesday morning and spent that day getting things in order and had a desk full of matter for correspondence to be dealt with on Thursday.

I had just reached the office yesterday morning, and was taking off my belt, when I heard an awful explosion which shook everything. Then came another one and I knew nothing more until I found myself on my hands and knees trying to get out from under the building, which had collapsed on top of us. I was cut on the head and hand in a number of places but, beyond that, was not hurt. I called to the man in the office with me to get out before the second bomb struck us, as I thought that an air raid was in progress.

We crawled out through the windows and everything was black. I had lost my glasses and could not see very far, but I could see that there was no airship above us. So I crawled back into the office again to get some money orders and cheques and took them over to the office of the Paymaster of the Composite Battalion, which was about 50 yards from me. I found it in ruins and, looking round, I saw that every window in the barracks had been broken and that men were beginning to appear from all quarters, terribly cut about the head and hands and some with broken arms and legs.

I went back to my own office and told my staff to let things alone there and to help with the wounded. The women and children from the married quarters now appeared on the scene in a pitiful state. Their houses were all broken up, the end being literally ripped off one of them and every roof caved in. I heard later that one woman had her eyes out and a child had the top of its head blown off. The conditions were appalling.

One of our men had been thrown 25 yards from the building and was lying on the ground in agony from internal injuries. I got a couple of first-aid men to take him away and was moving over to the gate, to see what could be done for the women and children, when I looked behind and saw a fire starting in our building. I called to my staff and we all piled inside to save the records but it was of no use. We had to clear out with a comparatively few papers and the place was gone in ten minutes—with all the records of the unit.

I went back to the gate and saw Captain Turner, our Quartermaster, carried out with broken thigh and fearful cuts to the head. I had managed to get my overcoat and flung it to one of my men, telling him we would go down to the Pay Office. When I looked round for him, he was gone with the coat and I was left there without coat or hat.

I asked the M.O. what I could do and he said he wanted blankets, so I got a crowd of men together and we raided stores and brought out a pile of greatcoats as there were no blankets left.

I then went across to the Officers' Quarters with Captain Brignell and found everything there in an awful state, though only one officer was badly injured.

The fire had, by this time, broken out all over the North End and we could see nothing but a blaze north of the barracks. St Mark's Church was a roaring furnace. I came back to the gate to look after my papers and as I was picking them up, a shout came to get away from all brick buildings as the magazine in the Dockyard had caught and was going to blow up. So, I started up the street in a private's greatcoat I had picked up, a civilian cap and with a bandaged head and face covered with blood, holding a bundle of papers in my hands.

I overtook one of the men from the Pay Office with his wife, one of them bleeding terribly, and helped them along and got them into a car. I was then near the Common so I kept on and found people congregated there in thousands. I went on till I got to Mrs Crawford's. I found that not a single pane of glass had been broken in my room. I washed off some of the blood and then went and reported to the Pay Office. Everything there was in confusion. I then went to a drug store on Barrington Street and had my cuts

Remains of the Richmond Printing building. The structure near Kaye and Young streets was constructed out of granite blocks but could not withstand the blast. Thirty-eight people at the building were killed, including one of the owners, David Orr.

dressed and, after dinner at the Club, such as we could get for ourselves, I went down to the Pay Office again and there received orders to report at Headquarters, from where we were sent to the North End to do anything we could.

I can't begin to tell you of the awful sights. Dead bodies laid out in rows, men's arms and legs sticking out of the burning debris, burned to the bone, and the whole North End nothing but charred embers.

The hospitals are all full. Five-hundred were sent to Windsor last night to be looked after. Every available place is being used to house the homeless. Families are separated and they have no idea yet who has been killed, though the estimate is more than 2,000. The place looks like a deserted city with its boarded windows and, to make matters worse, a fearful snow storm is raging now. The

117

whole thing turns one's heart sick. They say some of the cases in the hospitals are dreadful. Every second person you see has been cut with glass.

Wellington Barracks is in an awful condition. The Officers' Mess looks as though it were a cardboard box which had been stepped on, but the men's quarters are intact except for the windows. The married quarters, as I have told you, are practically demolished.

I lost over $100.00 worth of stuff; my typewriter, desk, documents' case and some clothes; but I was lucky to escape with my life. If I had been five minutes earlier I would have been sitting at my desk and the wall would have fallen on my back and thrown me across the desk. Hugh was in the Club when it happened and escaped with a scratch on the head.

You have nothing to worry about as far as we are concerned. Everything is, of course, upside down. As I was writing this last sentence word came in of six of our men who have been killed.

Love to all,
Cuthbert

The military units in Halifax, comprised for the most part of militia battalions that had been called out for active service in 1914 in defence of the port, were to really prove themselves in the days following the explosion.

Apart from making up a number of the search and rescue parties, the troops were called upon for a hundred and one other duties. It was the military who provided many of the patrols that worked alongside the police to preserve law and order, and who supplied and pitched the tents on the Common that gave temporary shelter to hundreds of the injured and homeless.

When the snow storm blew up with all its ferocity, and it was realized that the people living out on the Common would probably not survive it under such exposed conditions, the soldiers marched out of their barracks and turned them over to the victims of the disaster whilst they went under canvas.

Typifying the spirit of the army at this time was the report that a single detail of the 63rd Halifax Rifles worked as a rescue party all day and then mounted guard all night, in arctic temperatures, for seventy-two hours, without rest and without any defaulters.

Lillian had not been asleep for more than a few minutes when a sound outside the barrack room woke her. She sat up, listening, and then she heard it again, a hesitant shuffle followed by a low, strangled moan. The shuffling grew louder until she knew that whatever was making the noise was only just out of sight. Then a wildly flung hand found the doorpost and gripped it fiercely, and a man pulled himself into view and stood framed in the doorway.

Although his uniform was in tatters and coated with filth and dust, Lillian could see that he was a soldier. He took one step into the room, his free hand groping in the air before him, and the girl saw his face. She had witnessed many horrors that day, but now she had difficulty in suppressing a scream.

The man's hair had been burned away and his scalp was one suppurating, open blister that crowned his head like a skullcap. On the left side of his face, his lower jaw, from the ear to the centre of his mouth, was missing, and where his nose should have been there was now only a bloody smudge and tendrils of torn flesh. Both his eye sockets were empty, and from one of them there dangled an eyeball that tapped against his cheek when he moved.

The terrified girl drew back on the bed silently, gagging herself with her knuckles. For a minute or two the soldier stood in the doorway, cocking his head from side to side like an animal, as if trying to detect any sound of movement, and one hand, with the fingers spread wide, circled in a desperate, blind search. From time to time the wreck of his mouth trembled and he let

119

out a piteous moan that seemed to come from deep inside him. Then he would cock and twist his head again, listening for some response to his cry, but Lillian could not bring herself to speak, and in a little while the soldier shuffled away.

When, at last, her two friends returned, they said that they had not been able to find anyone in the barracks who could help her, but they had learned that there was a car leaving shortly for Camp Hill Hospital and the driver had agreed to take her there.

Lillian thanked them, and then she told them about the man in the doorway. For what seemed a long time, no one spoke, but then one of the soldiers triumphantly produced an apple pie, which he broke into pieces, and they all sat on the bed and ate hungrily.

The soldiers went with her to the car when it was time for her to leave. They promised they would come and see her at the hospital just as soon as they could, and then the car started moving and the two waving figures were soon out of sight.

Lillian reached Camp Hill Hospital just after the last bottle of anesthetic had been used, and only shortly before the final length of gut had been knotted on a wound. Supplies of every other type of surgical equipment and of most drugs had been exhausted even earlier, and for many hours the doctors were to operate, without gloves, on conscious patients, and to stitch their incisions with ordinary cotton thread.

The hospital was swamped with casualties. There were no beds available when Lillian arrived, and any system of registration had long since broken down, so that, with dozens of others, she wandered through the wards until she found a clear space on the floor, and then she sat down and waited for treatment.

Around her lay the dead and the dying, and along the corridor immediately opposite her, three doctors, sharing one set of instruments, were operating simultaneously on patients who screamed and struggled on top of wooden tables stained red with blood.

The operations went on without a pause. As one patient was lifted off a table, having had an eye removed or a leg or arm amputated, so another was trundled or carried over to it, and the surgeon began again.

Throughout the afternoon, more and more volunteer nurses flooded into the hospital, but there were never enough to cope with the steady flow of admissions, and for many of the injured, the most that could be provided was a hasty dressing applied by untrained hands.

From time to time, soldiers, acting as orderlies, would sort through those people stretched out on the floor and remove the dead to make room for others.

Lillian waited all through that afternoon for attention, but no one came near her. Then, a little before six in the evening, one of the doctors beckoned to her to come over, and she got up and went to him.

"Can you stand all right?" he asked.

Lillian nodded.

"Use your arms?"

"One of them's cut a bit," she replied.

"You'll do," he announced. "Come with me." He led her down the corridor to one of the wooden tables, onto which a nurse and a male orderly were lifting the naked body of a girl whose face and shoulders were covered with blood.

The orderly took hold of the girl's arms at the elbow joints and, pushing Lillian forward, the doctor said in a tired voice, "Take her legs and hold 'em tight. I'm going to remove one of her eyes, and there's nothing I can give her." Then he picked up a scalpel and began to operate.

As the knife cut into her, the patient on the table screamed loudly, and Lillian had to lie over her knees to hold her down.

Within seconds, though, the girl had passed out, and by the time she came round again it was all over, and a nurse was washing the blood from her face. Then, for the first time, Lillian recognized her as the girl who had been working the machine next to her when the cotton factory had fallen apart around them, so long—it seemed so long—ago.

Later that evening, Lillian's own wounds were dressed and she was eventually put to bed on a mattress laid out on the floor. She slept fitfully, though, and once when she woke early on Friday morning, she saw through the window that it was snowing hard.

On Monday, December 10, Lillian Atkins was driven to the railway station to catch a train that would take her to her hometown of Yarmouth. As she stood on the platform, drinking a cup of coffee thrust into her hand by a friendly, fussing Red Cross worker, she caught sight of her reflection in a carriage window.

It took her some few seconds to accept the fact that the white-faced, bandaged apparition with the long, uncombed hair, thickly matted with blood, that gazed back at her from the glass was herself. Then she realized that she had left the hospital still wearing the army greatcoat that one of the two young soldiers had lent her four days earlier.

Her immediate reaction was that somehow she must return it, and she started to take it off, intending to give it to the woman from the Red Cross with a note. But then she remembered that she did not know his name, and so she boarded the train and went home, taking with her an outsize present from a friendly stranger.

When Cadet Brock saw the extent of the damage outside the dockyard, he realized that he must return to the college at once.

Turning, he headed back through the gate at a trot, and when he reached the lawn again he found that many of his classmates had already re-gathered there after their momentary panic, and that others were coming in from all directions.

Numerous fires were burning in the dockyard, and from time to time, clouds of black smoke drifted through the assembly in front of the college. The senior instructor, Commander Howley, was supporting himself against the railings by the main entrance to the now battered and windowless building, engaged in urgent consultation with other members of the staff. Bewildered and excited, the boys stood around in groups, talking quietly.

Less than an hour earlier the cadets had been fussing and fretting over their appearance for the morning inspection. Now, in crumpled and torn uniforms powdered with dust, and, with few exceptions, with faces stained red or streaked with blood, they were hardly recognizable.

Although shocked and horrified by the spectacle, Brock at first found himself seized by an almost uncontrollable desire to laugh. But the moment of hysteria passed, and he went over to join his friends.

When a party of seniors carrying the two inert bodies appeared in the doorway of the college, everyone stopped talking and turned to watch.

"It's Mackenzie and CPO King," someone whispered.

"They found them in the lab!"

Gently, the unconscious petty officer and the young cadet were carried down the steps and laid, side by side, on the grass. Mackenzie's face was thickly crusted with blood and plaster so that his features were barely discernible, but they had wrapped King's head in a cloth so that his terrible wounds should not be seen.

When the rest of the seriously wounded had been brought out of the building, Commander Howley ordered those seniors who were only slightly hurt to get them down to the naval hospital. "The remainder of you," he said, "return to your quarters and pack all your belongings."

Amid the wreckage of their gunroom, Brock and the other juniors crammed their clothes and the contents of desks and lockers into trunks or suitcases in a hubbub of conversation. At first the boys talked gravely about the explosion and its terrible effect, but then someone pointed out that at least it had saved them from the dreaded end-of-term exams, and they cheered wildly and everyone shook hands.

They were still congratulating each other when one of the seniors almost fell into the room. "Commander's orders," he shouted. "Leave all your stuff, and get clear of the building and out of the dockyard in double-quick time. The magazine's on fire. Make for open ground. Right, jump to it!"

Bareheaded, Brock snatched his civilian cap from the trunk he had been packing and then raced for the door with the other juniors, who pounded down the corridor and out of the front entrance in a body.

Outside in the dockyard, it seemed as though everyone was running, and the cadets ran with them, now and then stopping for a second, exchanging a word or two, leaving one friend and falling in with another. As he streaked along, Brock saw that there was great confusion on all sides. Whilst some of the officers and sailors searched desperately for anyone who could confirm what orders had been given, others joined the flight to safety, and, gathering strength with every yard, the dark blue tide surged on toward the south gate.

When it spilled through the archway and out onto the road beyond, it was, on the instant, swallowed up as a tributary by a vast, swiftly flowing river of humanity.

"Flee!...Flee!" had been the cry of the soldiers throughout the city. "Get into open ground, the magazine is burning!" And the people did not need a second warning.

Up from cellars, down from towers, out from shops and offices and houses they had poured. The aged, the young, the sick, the wounded, the rich, and the poor. Society matron and prostitute; blacksmith and banker; clergyman and bootlegger; tinker and tailor; soldier and sailor. By their hundreds, by their thousands, terror stricken, intent, silent or screaming, they had come together under the banner of panic in answer to the one rallying cry: "Flee! Flee! Get into open ground!"

Behind them lay vacated homes, wide-open stores, churches without priests, and the trapped, the crippled, the maimed, and the entombed, who cried and begged for aid to the empty air.

For Brock, caught up in the midst of the exodus, it was an almost unbelievable sight. It seemed to him as though the whole population of Halifax was on the move. A single, broad column that stretched for miles, and which blocked the way for ambulances and fire engines speeding north.

Old men hobbling on crutches; young men running, pushing, clawing; mothers hugging tiny babies; mothers dragging stumbling, weeping children by the hand. Some carried bundles of hastily snatched up treasures, the majority had not dared to stop for anything. Hundreds rode in crawling vehicles, thousands were on foot. And when the call had come, they had fled as they were.

There were bakers in aprons; clergymen in cassocks; women in nightdresses; men in shirt sleeves; children in bare feet. Many were scantily clothed, and some of those who had dragged themselves from the ruins of their homes, black-red with blood and dirt, or who had been raped by the blast, were naked, uncaring, and unmindful of the cold.

With blanched faces, bleeding bodies, and bellies full of fear, and with seldom a backward glance, on, on they pressed toward the sanctuary of the open spaces; to the Common, to the fields, to the parks, but mostly to Citadel Hill.

Able Seaman Lawson clambered over the debris and dropped down into a narrow zigzag path which was all that remained of the road. He had lost the others in the rescue party early on and now he was trying to find them again.

"Hey, Jack!"

Lawson spun round to see who was calling. Away to his left, in a patch of open ground, a sailor, sitting with his back against the roots of a broken stone wall, was beckoning him over.

When he got close, Lawson saw that he was a middle-aged man, and obviously a regular with years of service in the Royal Navy behind him. Strewn around were a dozen or more empty beer bottles, and six or seven boxes were stacked by his side. In the fingers of his right hand he held a cigar with exaggerated daintiness.

"Oh, you're a young 'un," the man said in a disappointed tone, but then added, "Still, never mind. Well, sit down, boy."

Lawson sank down beside him.

"What ship you off, then?" the old sweat enquired.

"*Niobe*. But I'm only there till my orders come through."

"Good luck! Smoke?" A large box of cigars was thrust under Lawson's nose. The seventeen-year-old sailor recoiled a little and shook his head. "No thanks, they don't agree with me." His companion laughed and whipped the cigars away. "Have some chocolate then." He selected another box from the pile at his side and opened it. It was filled with dozens of bars of chocolate. "Here you are," he said. "Catch!" He tossed a handful of them to Lawson.

The boy thanked him and, settling himself back against the wall, tore the paper from one of the bars and bit into it.

"You with one of the rescue parties?"

"I was to start with," the older man chuckled, drawing deeply on his cigar, "But then I slipped off to do a bit of rescuing on my own, if you follow me." He patted the boxes beside him, and gave Lawson a broad wink through a cloud of smoke. Suddenly the chocolate went sour with the thought of the penalty for looting. The sailor from the *Niobe* changed the subject quickly.

"Where are all the people who live round here, then? I've been walking for a quarter of an hour or more and I haven't seen anybody. They weren't all killed, were they?"

"No! They've gone up the Common. Won't do 'em no good, though. When it goes up, the whole of Nova Scotia will go up with it."

Bewildered, Lawson exclaimed, "But it's already gone up."

His new-found friend hawked loudly, and then spat expertly onto one of the beer bottles. "Not the ship! I'm talking about the magazine. It's on fire, and they expect it to blow up any minute. That's why everyone's gone up the Common, see? Bloody fools! If your number's up, your number's up, and that's all there is to it. It's no use running away, is it?"

The bars of chocolate spilled from his lap as Lawson got to his feet. "No, of course not. You're so right," he said casually, with a laugh, taking out his handkerchief to wipe away the perspiration that had suddenly broken out on his brow; and then he blurted, "Tell me something, will you?"

"Of course I will, boy." The old sweat took the cigar from his mouth and looked up at him, surprised by the urgency in his voice. "What do you want to know?"

"Which way's the Common?"

When, in their wild panic, the people of Halifax fled from their homes and stores, leaving them unguarded and unlocked, the looters, who were already at work turning over the wreckage and rifling the corpses, moved in.

There was little risk of arrest, for the few harassed policemen in the city could not possibly be everywhere, and the military

Destroyed house in Halifax's North End. Destruction was most severe in the Richmond area of the North End and across the harbour in Dartmouth around Tufts Cove.

and naval cordons and patrols had not yet appeared on the scene.

Dwight Johnston, who lived through the disaster, later wrote in his journal,

"Few folk thought that Halifax harbored any would-be ghouls or vultures. The disaster showed how many. Men clambered over the bodies of the dead to get beer in the shattered breweries. Men taking advantage of the flight from the city because of the possibility of another explosion went into houses and shops, and took whatever their thieving fingers could lay hold of.

"Then there were the nightly prowlers among the ruins, who rifled the pockets of the dead and dying, and snatched rings from icy fingers.

"A woman lying unconscious on the street had her fur coat snatched from her back...One of the workers, hearing someone groaning rescued a shopkeeper from underneath the debris. Unearthing at the same time a cash box containing $150, he gave it to a young man standing by to hold while he took the victim to a place of refuge.

"When he returned the box was there, but the young man and the money had disappeared."

Of the looters who struck when large areas of the city were deserted, few were caught, but of these, some were unluckier than others in their choice of victim.

When the call to evacuate was shouted along Queen and up Fenwick Streets, Mrs. Satchell, a muscular Irishwoman with the shoulders and strength of a man, who owned the corner candy store, joined the throng heading for Citadel Hill. She was halfway there before she remembered that she had not locked the shop and, her concern overcoming her fear, she turned back.

The man was filling a washing basket with her stock when Mrs. Satchell came up behind him. He saw her and, turning, threw the basket at her and tried to run out of the store. She brought him down with a single blow that broke his jaw. Then she draped the senseless looter over her shoulder, carried him out into the street, and dumped him at the feet of the first policeman she met.

Once the police had been reinforced with armed patrols made up of militiamen mounted and, on foot, Royal Marines, and later, sailors from the American cruisers *Tacoma* and *Von Steuben,* the devastated area was cordoned off, and orders issued that any looter trying to escape was to be shot.

Although Chief of Police Hanrahan was later to deny vehemently, at least in public, rumours that these orders had more than once been carried out, the fact is that six men were killed resisting arrest by service patrols.

There were many sensational and often lurid stories circulating at the time of the disaster concerning the shooting of looters, but none of them was ever substantiated with evidence.

One such story, however, has since been corroborated to a very great extent by independent and reliable witnesses. It first appeared in a Toronto newspaper on December 11, 1917, and on the following day was reprinted in part and attacked in the *Halifax Herald.*

BETTER STICK NEARER TO TRUTH

A Toronto newspaper yesterday carried a story with a heading which announced that in Halifax on the previous day "One looter was shot, his body strapped to a post, over which was affixed a flaming legend which stated: 'This was a looter.'" While there is an announced determination on the part of the military authorities to shoot looters in the devastated district, there has been nothing to justify the picturesque story of the Toronto correspondent. Surely there is sufficient "copy" in the facts of the present situation to make unnecessary the exercise of the inventive genius of some of our visiting correspondents.

Typical of the corroboration available for this story is an extract from a letter written by Richard M. Lee, who in 1917 was a junior engineer officer on board HMS *Columbella* of the Tenth Cruiser Squadron. The *Columbella* put into Halifax very shortly after the disaster, and relief parties were landed to give assistance.

In his letter, Lee describes what he saw when he went ashore with a brother officer, and although his account of this incident differs in some ways from that printed in the Toronto newspaper, in essence the similarity is too great to be ignored. Lee's version of the story has since been borne out in every important detail by other eyewitnesses.

I was in the devastated area some few days after the explosion with a shipmate, it was afternoon, dark and desolate. I stooped to pick up a twisted fragment of steel as a souvenir and my companion said, "You B.F., watch out or you'll be shot. Look!"

To the north was the tottering remains of a sugar refinery. To the west, the lone figure of a soldier silhouetted against the grey sky on a horse, motionless and with a carbine across his saddle. Not a living thing anywhere in sight besides us three, a silence you could feel, the snow everywhere, the leaden waters of the tragic harbour alongside.

Across on the farther shore low, snow covered, scowling hills with sombre pines.

Towards the sugar refinery I looked again and said, "A crucifix, look! Full size. I wonder who put that up?" My companion replied, "That's not a crucifix. It is a looter shot and strapped to a door."

I did not go to see it, it was some distance away; it was dusk and I had had enough of the awful place.

When "Billy" Brock got onto Citadel Hill, its slopes were black with thousands of terrified people. Picking his way carefully through the crowd, he moved upward toward the walls of the fortress so as to get a better view.

The ashen faced refugees, some massed in groups, some singly, some running anxiously back and forth like ants when their hill has been crushed, waited, cold and hungry, for the second great explosion, and whilst they waited many of them fell on their knees and prayed.

As he walked among them, Brock caught snatches of wild rumours that spread like forest fires around the hill. "The Germans have landed in Purcell's Cove and the Militia's calling for volunteers..." "Fifty U-boats, that's what he said. Saw them with his own eyes..." "And they had the dynamite on them. Going to hang them, they are." "...Have you heard? There's not a living soul in Dartmouth." "...Came ashore in a little boat just before dawn and asked for a glass of water in German!"

Later, doctors were to compile and analyze the hallucinations that many Haligonians experienced at this time. More than one person reported, and genuinely believed, that following the explosion, they had looked up into the sky and seen a Zeppelin. A man living in Dartmouth heard the "shells" scream over him just before the detonation, and another citizen witnessed the entire German fleet manoeuvring out at sea. Several described in every detail faces that they had seen in the great column of smoke, and which had remained visible for some considerable time.

From the summit of the hill, Brock could see much of the city spread below him, bathed in bright sunshine.

The harbour was alive with activity, and vessels of all kinds—steamers, schooners, tugs, sailing boats, and many warships—were under way, steaming down to other, safer berths, or manoeuvring to anchor in mid-channel. The white sails of the small boats stood out against the blue of the water and the green of the Dartmouth hills.

To the north, the totally devastated area was hidden from view by buildings, and by the smoke and flames belching up from what seemed, at that height, to be an unbroken sea of fire.

For more than two hours the thousands who had gathered on the hill waited, but there was no explosion, and eventually soldiers came up from the city in trucks and announced, through megaphones, that the danger was over. Slowly the people dispersed, leaving the hillside trampled and scarred.

During the afternoon Brock went back to the college, and after a welcome meal of bread, cheese, and milk, eaten in the senior gunroom, he finished his packing. Later the cadets were told that they were to find billets in the town for themselves. For many this was not easy, but Brock was lucky in having friends in Halifax who gladly took him in.

He stayed with them for three days, and worked as a messenger in the City Hall. But on the Monday following the disaster, he left for Vancouver, and Christmas at home.

The train pulled slowly out of the almost demolished station, where men were still at work clearing the debris, past the dockyard, past the blue waters of the Narrows, and through the desolate North End. Here, there was nothing standing as far as the eye could see. The ground was, as a major in the carriage remarked, "In the same condition as land that has been under constant shellfire for a month."

Gazing through the window, Brock could scarcely tell where the streets had run and the houses had stood, but then the train gathered speed, and, leaving the horror behind it, drew into clear, clean country.

Mr. Strickland's Academy on Morris Street was not badly hit by the blast, but the windows had been blown in, and several of the boys had been cut. When Trevor Frowd arrived, some of the parents who took their sons to school were still there, dressing wounds.

No one seemed to have a very clear idea of what had happened, nor of how serious the damage was in the North End.

But it was obvious that, without a window in the building, the school would have to close, for a time anyway. Mr. Strickland announced a special holiday, and said that the term would recommence on Monday, December 10.

On his way back along Morris Street, Trevor overtook a younger boy whom he knew slightly, who was walking with his mother. He fell in with them, and the two boys talked excitedly.

They went down till they reached Barrington Street and then, almost without warning, they were caught up in the great flood running from the threat of another explosion.

For a time they were swept along, running in its midst, but eventually the boy's mother managed to get them a lift on a baker's "team," and the driver took them to Point Pleasant Park.

More than three thousand wretched, panic-stricken people had taken refuge in the park, which lay on the southernmost tip of the peninsula.

They sheltered among the trees and bushes, and some of them cut down branches and lit fires, for it was very cold. Lying uncovered in the centre of one huddled group, an hysterical woman, seven months pregnant, gave birth to a boy. The baby lived for only a few minutes, but when they told the woman it was dead, she would not believe them. Wrapping it in a woollen scarf, she cradled it in her arms, and when she fell asleep they took it away and buried it in the sand down by the water's edge.

When the soldiers on horseback rode through the park shouting that the danger was over, Trevor Frowd went home.

The walls of No. 8 The Dockyard leaned inward and most of the roof had been sliced away, but his parents had not been injured, and his mother cried a great deal when she saw him.

And in the evening, Trevor's dog turned up.

A search and rescue party from *Changuinola* found Edith O'Connell, and the child was conscious when they picked her up.

She was laid on a mattress and put on board a naval tug that took her down to the dockyard jetty, and from there she was transferred by ambulance to hospital.

By the time she arrived, however, she was unconscious again, and after the doctors had examined her they rushed her into the operating theatre. For six days Edith lay in a coma, but on the sixth day her eyes flickered open and she could see, and the doctors knew then that she would recover.

As soon as news of the disaster reached the Royal Flying Corps squadron in which Edith's father, Arthur O'Connell, was serving, he was granted compassionate leave.

When he arrived in Halifax, he hurried to the house on Campbell Road only to find that it no longer existed; and in the Chebucto Road mortuary he identified the bodies of his mother, his three brothers, his two sisters, his wife, and his two younger children. He was told that, although her body had not been recovered, it was almost certain that Edith, too, had been killed, and that only by a miracle could she have survived.

When he had buried his family, Arthur O'Connell went away from Halifax, and the seven-year-old girl, then lying unconscious and unidentified in hospital, was never to see him again.

Kenneth Mackenzie began to come round as the senior cadets lifted him into the handcart. He had great difficulty in seeing, but as the cart was trundled away from the college, he could just make out from the man's uniform that it was CPO King, his head swathed in a blood soaked cloth, who lay motionless beside him.

The cadets pushed the cart out of the dockyard and up toward Admiralty House, which some time earlier had been converted into a hospital and clinic. When they reached it, though, the building was on fire and they found that casualties were being routed to other hospitals.

Mackenzie and King were taken off the cart and put into the back of a lorry loaded with injured men, women, and children. The lorry was driven to Camp Hill Hospital, where the walking cases alighted first, and then orderlies came out with stretchers for the remainder. The cadet was carried into the chaos and confusion of the wards and put to bed.

When the orderlies came back for King, though, and saw his covered face, before moving him, one of them took his pulse and, unable to detect a heartbeat, certified him as dead. "This one's for Chebucto," he told the driver.

Although the building had been damaged, within two or three hours of the disaster, the military had patched Chebucto Road School sufficiently for it to be pressed into service as a mortuary.

In the days that followed, a seemingly unbroken procession of people seeking relatives or friends made their way to the school, to file through row upon row of bodies that lay under white sheets on trestle tables.

It was a little after 1:00 P.M. on the Thursday that William King was brought in. His body was stripped and tagged, set down among the hundreds of others, and covered with a sheet.

On Saturday, the chief petty officer regained consciousness.

His mind cleared quickly, but he found he could not see; neither could he move; neither could he speak. So that, although he could hear movement around him, he had no way of attracting attention.

In a little while, footsteps approached and stopped where he lay. Something that covered his face was lifted away and there was silence for a moment. "No, that's not him," a man said, and the cover was dropped back again. The footsteps faded away, and King realized where he was.

For three more hours he lay, a living corpse among the dead in the icy chill of the mortuary, desperately willing movement into his limbs. Twice the sheet was pulled from his face again, and he struggled to speak, to smile, to turn his head; but he could not, and the searchers passed on down the line.

Then he heard someone walking, and the footsteps got nearer and nearer. King was certain that whoever it was would pass close by him. Concentrating all his thoughts onto his right arm, he managed to spread his fingers a little. But it was hardly perceptible, and the footsteps were now at his side and soon they would be gone. With a supreme effort he tried again and, in a flurry of white sheet, his arm shot out like a spring, his fingers closed on rough material, and the soldier walking past the end table let out a scream.

William King was alive again.

It was from some of the dozens of injured who converged on Dr. Dickinson's house that Bessie Fraser learnt the true cause of the explosion. For a while she helped Mrs. Dickinson to roll bandages and prepare dressings, but then her husband came looking for her and they took the children home.

Alex told her of the appalling destruction and of the fires raging in Richmond, and from their back door they could see that Dartmouth, too, had suffered terribly.

North of the skating rink, which had collapsed in a heap, whole streets had been levelled and, as across the water, fires had broken out which, unchecked, were now spreading rapidly.

Oland's Brewery, almost opposite the point of the explosion, and with nothing between it and the water's edge but the railway tracks, had been totally demolished by the blast, and the tracks were blocked by wreckage. Of the Consumers Cordage Company's rope works, nothing remained but two cracked and tottering walls and a mountainous pile of bricks.

The report that the magazine was in danger was heliographed from Halifax, and before long the Frasers were warned to leave their house. They took cover in an open field until they were told it was safe to return.

By now the wounded were being brought out from the northern end of the town, which had taken the worst of the blast, and with no hospital available and few buildings of any size still standing, the doctors were operating on tables set out on the sidewalk. Later, the serious cases were to be taken to Halifax by boat.

During the afternoon, Alex moved his family in with his parents, with whom they were to stay until their house was repaired.

As she was collecting together their belongings, Bessie looked about her shattered home. She realized for the first time just how much of that which was precious to them all they had lost, and she wanted to cry. But then she saw the pram, and she remembered, and suddenly the splintered furniture, the broken ornaments, the ruined clothes, and the damaged roof and walls just weren't important any more.

As the water receded around him, John Gammon crawled over to the helpless, choking divers and unscrewed their face glasses. Hungrily they took in deep gulps of fresh air, and when they had recovered a little, the master-at-arms shouted to Critch, who he could see struggling free of the dripping wreckage of the pump shelter, to come over and help him remove their suits.

When this was done, Gammon turned his attention to the three sailors lying further up the pier, but here there was nothing he could do; they were all dead.

As he straightened up from them, he saw the flames rising from Richmond, and for the first time he thought of his home on Union Street, of his wife and two babies who would be there now, and of Dorothy and Ena May at school. Suddenly he was afraid, and, ordering Able Seaman Critch to take over and look after the divers, he hurried off across the dockyard.

Gammon made his way along Campbell Road, and as he walked, the heat from the burning buildings on all sides dried his dripping clothing within minutes. As he got further and further into the devastated area, though, the heat became so unbearable that he put up the hood of his duffle coat to shield his face.

It took him a very long time to find Union Street and his demolished house, but only a second to realize the impossibility of anyone being alive in it. Sick at heart and stumbling over burning debris, stopping now and then to take his bearings, he pressed on to Gottingen Street and St. Joseph's School.

The roof and two walls of the school had collapsed inwards, and the bodies of several children lay in the street before it, but neither Dorothy nor Ena May was among them.

In the doorway sat a small girl, her hands and face cut by glass and her clothes soaked with blood. Gammon tore a piece from his shirt, and with that and his handkerchief he bound up her wounds as best he could. And then he asked her if she knew his daughters, but she said she didn't, and he went on up the steps and into the building.

The scene inside was one of utter confusion, with terrified children running in all directions through thickly strewn rubble, whilst two or three frantic nuns tried to get them together. Sister Edwina, who the master-at-arms knew well, was not among them, and when he asked one of the nuns if she had seen her or his children, she shook her head.

It was impossible to reach the upper stories, as the stairway was blocked, but Gammon searched the ground floor thoroughly without success.

As he came slowly out of the school and stood on the top step, he heard someone scream his name, and looking up, he saw a woman whom he recognized as his next door neighbour break away from two soldiers who were helping her into a truck, and race across to him.

He went down the steps to meet her, and she grabbed his arm and cried hysterically, "Oh Mr. Gammon, it's no good, they've gone. Mrs. Gammon and the children, they've all gone. I saw them die."

The first lieutenant was on deck when the chief master-at-arms returned on board *Niobe*. The officer hardly recognized him. He seemed, all at once, to have got much older. His face was drained of colour and void of expression, and when he spoke to him, Gammon gave him only a blank, unknowing stare and wandered aimlessly away along the deck.

Early the next day, Gammon received news that his seven-year-old daughter, Dorothy, was, in fact, alive and well, and that she was being cared for by a family in town. Only a few hours later, Ena May, aged five, was accounted for in a note from the Mother Superior of Mount St. Vincent Convent, which said the child had been found wandering on the street some miles from St. Joseph's School. She, too, was reported to be well.

Overjoyed, Gammon now allowed himself to hope that the day might also bring news of his wife and the other two children. But he heard nothing more, and so, on Friday, December 8, he placed an advertisement in the *Evening Mail*.

MISSING

From 39 1/2 Union Street
Mrs. Maude Gammon
Freddie Gammon, 3 years
Laura Gammon, 14 months
Any trace of same please communicate to
Mr. Gammon, Chief M.A.A., *Niobe*.

There was no response.

On Saturday, however, hope was revived again when a friend pointed out to him, in the daily list of casualties admitted to the hospitals, a small boy with a surname so similar that he felt sure there was a good chance it was a misprint, and that it was, in fact, Gammon's son, Freddie.

The chief master-at-arms went immediately to the hospital to which the boy had been admitted. When he described his son to the nurse who interviewed him, he was told that their patient could easily be Freddie. But when she took him into the ward, he saw that he was not, and he shook his head and turned to leave.

At the door, the nurse called him back and asked him if he were trying to trace anyone else. When he said he was, she told him that she had been present at an operation, earlier that day, on a woman with the same name as his.

Steeling himself in advance for a further disappointment, Gammon asked to be taken to the woman. He approached the bed apprehensively and saw his wife, badly injured and semi-conscious, but alive.

Of Freddie and the baby, Laura, there was never any news.

CHAPTER EIGHT
DAYS OF RESCUE AND RELIEF

"**M**ost deeply regret to hear of serious explosion at Halifax, resulting in great loss of life and property. Please convey to the people of Halifax, where I have spent so many happy times, my true sympathy in this grievous calamity."
—George, R.I.

Within thirty minutes of the explosion, organized search and rescue parties were at work amongst the wreckage, digging out the dead and the injured.

By 4:00 P.M. the city fire department had the blaze in Richmond under control, and twelve hours later the fires were out, except in a few isolated and contained areas where, despite all efforts, the debris continued to smoulder and burn for many days.

Long before sunset on that black Thursday, a military cordon had been thrown around the devastation, and patrols were out on the streets. And by lunchtime on the following day, a relief committee had been set up and was already at work.

The immediate task was to provide aid for the injured, shelter for the homeless, and food for the hungry. The committee set about solving these problems with energy and imagination.

The work of relief and rescue was made immeasurably more difficult by the blizzard that howled over the city, burying the ruins and the trapped, causing untold suffering among the homeless, and disrupting all traffic. Then came the floods and the ice to add further torment.

But Halifax was not alone in her moment of trial. Offers of money and relief came pouring in, not only from other parts of Canada, but from all over the world. New Zealand made a grant of $50,000, and Australia sent $250,000. The Canadian government voted $19,000,000 in all, and Britain pledged $5,000,000. The Lord Mayor of London opened a fund that closed at $600,000. New York held a special Halifax Relief Day and raised $75,000, and Chicago cabled $130,000. Altogether the contributions amounted to close on $30,000,000.

The generosity of many countries was great, but it was from the United States of America that the first and most valuable assistance came. At nine o'clock on the Thursday night, a special train left Boston with a large quantity of medical supplies, and on the following day a second train pulled out containing full equipment for a five-hundred-bed hospital and twenty-five doctors, two obstetricians, sixty-eight nurses, and eight orderlies.

At 1:00 P.M. on that same day, a Halifax relief train left New York City with five hundred cots, eighteen thousand garments, ten thousand blankets, twenty cases of disinfectants, one hundred and sixty cases of surgical supplies, a carload of foodstuffs, and more doctors and social workers.

Help came from all over America. It came by rail and it came by sea.

On Saturday, December 8, the SS *Calvin Austin* sailed from Boston with a vast cargo of supplies, including much needed glass, but bad weather delayed her and she arrived only a little ahead of the SS *Northland,* the second relief steamer dispatched from the same port.

The arrival of these steamers caused great excitement in Halifax, particularly that of the *Northland,* which was reported at length in the *Morning Chronicle.*

Steaming closely behind the *Calvin Austin* and arriving here not twenty-four hours later, the steamer *Northland* entered the port of Halifax yesterday morning bearing a cargo valued at $150,000, sent by the people of Massachusetts to the relief of the people of Halifax.

Mr. John F. O'Connell, a member of the Massachusetts Halifax Relief Committee, came in charge of the party, with instructions to hand the cargo over to the Relief Committee here. There also came four nurses from the Massachusetts Eye and Ear Infirmary at Boston. When it became known that there were such a large number of patients who suffered with their eyes and ears it was decided to send nurses with training for that work...

One of the most interesting portions of the *Northland's* cargo is the ten motor trucks, which have been presented as an absolute gift to the City of Halifax by the State of Massachusetts. Those trucks are of the finest makes, and show an expenditure of over $25,000. On the sides of each truck are signs reading, 'Massachusetts to Halifax'. There are included five Republics, three Whites and two Stewarts. Ten drums of gasoline also accompanied these trucks, as it was not known in Boston whether gasoline was plentiful here or not.

Each truck has a chauffeur, who will stay here until local men are trained and able to man the trucks. These chauffeurs are all Bostonians. When seen yesterday after the landing of the trucks, they proved to be an efficient looking, businesslike crew.

The trucks were landed from the steamer, now at Whitman's wharf, yesterday afternoon, and about six o'clock proceeded to a point in front of the Halifax Hotel, where they attracted a great deal of attention. Large numbers viewed the trucks and many

A party of children at one of the relief stations from which emergency supplies of food were issued to victims of the tragedy.

made minute inspection of them. It is expected that a parade will be held this morning of the ten trucks through the principal streets, before they start their relief work.

Besides the trucks, the *Northland* brought a large assortment of goods, which will be landed immediately. The following is a list of her cargo: 2084 packages of Beaver Board, 200 cases crackers, 510 packages second hand clothing, 51 kegs nails, 23 drums cement, 13 cases dry goods, 837 cases glass, 94 cases rubbers, 1045 cases boots and shoes, 1 keg fittings, 1 box glazier tools.

When the New York newspapers announced, two days after the explosion, that a blizzard was halting rescue work in Halifax, the Department of Civilian Relief of the American Red Cross had already dispatched a trainload of supplies and a group of skilled salvage men to assist in this work. To W. Frank Persons, director general of civilian relief, the coming of the blizzard meant one thing—death from exposure or from the slower processes of pneumonia. He therefore telegraphed to the authorities in Halifax, with whom he had previously been in touch, asking whether anti-pneumonia serum was needed.

It was not until 8:00 P.M. on the following day—Sunday—that the answer, "Thank you. Send one million units pneumoniac serum," reached him. But within fifteen minutes, the manager of the Atlantic Division of the Red Cross in New York City had been reached by telephone at his home and advised of the request. The names of half a dozen places in the United States where anti-pneumonia serum was made were given to him. Several of these were in New York, one in Philadelphia.

When the request for a million units was made to the manufacturers, they were amazed. Anti-pneumonia serum was a comparatively new product of preventive medicine. It was certainly not spoken of by the profession in terms of units, as was anti-diphtheria serum; moreover, a million units was declared to be an unheard of amount.

Three or four firms who were telephoned could not help. The fourth, a large firm of manufacturing chemists in Philadelphia, held out a slightly brighter hope. By noon on Monday, word had come from them that 850 ampoules of their anti-pneumococcal serum, or enough for several hundred patients, was available and could be dispatched that day. This quantity was, therefore, immediately purchased and by Monday evening was part of a trainload of other supplies that left New York, under the direction of the Red Cross, for Halifax.

The sending of this serum was only one of the dramatic and unusual incidents that occurred in the early days of meeting what was, and still is to this day, the greatest disaster ever to befall a Canadian city, and one of the greatest that has ever occurred in the western hemisphere. The prompt act of the Public Safety Committee of Massachusetts in sending, unbidden, not only a large quantity of glass and putty for broken windows but also twenty-five skilled glaziers to put it in, was another. The sending by the American Red Cross of a complete X-ray outfit with an operator accompanying it was a third.

In spite of the isolation of Halifax for several hours following the explosion, and the fact that, as is usual in large disasters, reliable details of the damage were not available, the Americans seemed to know exactly what would be needed, and throughout the country there were men and women willing and anxious to provide it.

And the people of Halifax have never forgotten the munificent and spontaneous aid that came from over the border, nor will they!

As the relief went on, the city slowly came to life again. Within an hour of the disaster one vital telegraph wire was working, and by the evening of the same day six direct multiplex wires had been established. Normal services were resumed a fortnight later.

The telephone system was very badly hit by the explosion and lost many of its operators. Nevertheless, limited lines, for emergency use only, were available on December 7, and from then on the situation steadily improved. The electricity supply was restored very quickly, but there was no flow of gas for three days, the gasometer having been wrecked.

When the smoke cleared, three miles of the main railway were buried under debris; North Street Station was almost a ruin, and rolling stock, valued at hundreds of thousands of dollars, had been shattered to pieces. In spite of this, a hospital train was sent out in the early afternoon of the disaster day, and incoming trains were switched to the new lines leading to the South End terminal. On the evening of the day following the disaster, the first regular train for Montreal left the city. Two days later the main lines were clear, and the first train pulled out of North Street Station on Saturday evening. By Monday the full passenger service was resumed, and eight days after the catastrophe all branches of the railway were working as normal.

Two or three trams were running again, on short routes, three hours after the explosion, but with the blizzard tying up all lines, it was not until the Sunday that it was possible to resume any semblance of a regular service.

The postal service was completely disorganized and was not resumed to any extent for four days, and it was weeks before there was a reliable distribution of mail. The banks, however, were open for business the morning after the catastrophe, just as soon as doors and windows had been replaced, and business went on as usual.

Although reduced in size for some time, there was no interruption to the daily issues of the newspapers, and the publishers, using hand compositors, were even able to produce limited single page editions for distribution on the day after the explosion.

Polling day for the city in the bitter general election campaign then in progress was deferred from December 17 to January 28, 1918, under the War Measures Act. The poll was later unnecessary, though, due to the withdrawal of the Liberal candidates.

To the delight of many children, there was no school until the following March.

The work of searching the wreckage went on day after day, and more and more bodies were brought out. Often the searchers would come across a body that could not be identified, or an arm, or a leg, or other remains, so that periodically the newspapers published, alongside the lists of casualties admitted to hospitals, column upon column of the gruesome details. These were closely studied by those with relatives still missing.

No. 438. Male. Fleece lined underwear. Black work shirt. Gold signet ring on third finger of left hand with initials R.B.W.

No. 441. Male. Age about 40 years. Brown hair, sandy moustache. Fleece lined underwear. Two cotton shirts. Grey heavy wool socks, striped grey pants.

No. 471. Female. Age about 4 years. Face completely disfigured. Light brown hair, blue sweater, black and white striped underwear, brown and black striped dress. Envelope found on body addressed Mrs. Julia Carroll, 1410 Barrington Street, City. Inside envelope receipt from Singer Sewing Machine Company, Halifax, issued 27 August, 1917.

No. C.524. Charred remains of body. Notation (All three brought in galvanised kettle with handle, marked from Campbell Road, about the orphanage, also marked Mr. and Mrs. Near and child.)

No. C.576. Charred remains of adult.

No. C.581. Charred remains taken from 41 North Albert Street, brought in old tin trunk.

No. 393. Female. Age about 45 years. Face disfigured. Cardboard on body with the following name: Mrs. Isabel Maldis. Black stockings, French high heel shoes, white corsets, medium weight underwear, one plain gold band ring on third finger of right hand.

No. 262. Male. Age about 38 years. Black hair, dark complexion. Dark grey heavy suit, dark grey sweater with collar, heavy ribbed underwear. Shirt with green and purple stripes. Soft collar. Fancy dark made-up tie, black socks and black overshoes. Pockets contained a twenty dollar bill, a small piece of paper, writing on which is indecipherable.

Exposed to the horror seen daily by relief and rescue workers, it is not surprising that some cracked. Dr. Shacknove, a young

Jewish doctor and one of the first medical men on the scene, was so affected by the terrible sights around him that he lost his mental balance completely. He was discovered dead one morning in his office. He had hanged himself during the night.

For a long time after the disaster all of those who had experienced it lived subconsciously on the knife-edge of panic, and twice, at least, thousands fled into the open country again on rumours of new dangers. Nor was the shock that many people had sustained immediately discernible. Six months after the explosion, the doctors of Halifax were inundated with people suffering, in varying degree, from inexplicable physical and mental breakdown.

Whilst the majority of Haligonians saw the disaster as a chance to give unstintingly of their time, money, and possessions in order to alleviate the distress, others saw it as a golden opportunity for profit.

Unscrupulous landlords raised rents astronomically. So much so that the Halifax Trades and Labour Council adopted a resolution that the mayor be authorized to request all persons to report landlords who "have taken advantage of conditions created by the explosion." For a time, when relief work was at its peak and hundreds of men and women were working twelve and fifteen hours a day without thought of payment, organized labour held the city to ransom.

Plumbers, quoting union rules, refused to work one minute beyond the regulation eight hours unless they received extra rates for overtime. The bricklayers, working on houses urgently needed for the homeless, would not allow plasterers to help in the repair of chimneys, and at the same time demanded higher rates and bonuses from the Relief Commission. One Halifax newspaper spoke of these men as "squeezing the uttermost farthing out of the anguished necessities of the homeless men, women and children." Truckmen charged exorbitant prices for carrying salvaged furniture and belongings. Some merchants boosted prices, but not always with success, as may be seen from this story in the *Halifax Herald*.

THE CHAUFFEUR DID RIGHT

It was reported to an alderman today that a small shopkeeper who asked of a little child 30 cents for a loaf of bread, was promptly thrashed by an auto chauffeur, who was in the shop at the time, and who handed the bread and some canned goods to the child.

On Tuesday, December 12, the deputy mayor issued a proclamation warning profiteers that they would be dealt with under the full provisions of the law.

Many of the prostitutes in the city moved back to Toronto or Montreal after the explosion, to return later when conditions had improved. For those who remained, though, business was brisk. The activities of the harbour were hardly interrupted and there was still a constant turnover of sailors and merchant seamen. There were customers, too, among the hundreds of building workers, of mixed nationalities, brought in to construct new houses.

With the appearance of these men, the crime rate for Halifax, already on the increase, shot up dramatically, and the city's detective force was hard pressed with investigations.

The prohibition law was not relaxed in any way during the crisis, and at the slightest hint of anyone dispensing the "demon" rum, the newspapers were ready with a pungent exposé and cry for action.

In spite of statements to the contrary, it has been proven that some few HUMAN FIENDS, PARASITES, AND GHOULS ROBBED DEAD BODIES AND RAIDED DESERTED HOUSES WITHIN A FEW HOURS OF THE GREAT EXPLOSION! And

NOW another danger threatens the city—a danger which must be handled at once and with the utmost possible rigor. IN THE MIDST OF THE CITY'S AGONY, WHILE THE DEAD BODIES OF HUNDREDS OF OUR CITIZENS LIE HEAPED IN GROUPS, scores and scores yet awaiting identification; with thousands of homes in mourning and the customary tenor of the city's life in a state of almost utter chaos—a notorious "bootlegger," who has long fooled the police and operated a "blind pig" within smell of police headquarters, has just forwarded $400 to Montreal for a new supply of booze, that he may continue his vile and nefarious business of "peddling poison" round our streets.

Only a totally depraved and sunken wretch would contemplate so hideous an act in the midst of this overwhelming crisis. It is easy to imagine the complete demoralisation and the very grave conditions which would inevitably follow the sale of booze poison in shattered Halifax today. "Booze" at the hour means added PERIL. It would be the direct avenue to looting, acts of lawlessness, and grave possibilities of fires. This matter must, for the safety of all concerned, be taken in hand and STOPPED at once.

First: Let the Ottawa government be advised of the seriousness of allowing liquor to be shipped into the province AT ALL during these days of crisis.

Second: Before the government has time to act, Mayor Martin should station men at the terminals to inspect all express packages coming into the city and—as an emergency measure—immediately CONFISCATE all liquor, save that directly ordered by the chairman of the relief committee for medicinal purposes.

Third: The Dominion Express Company and the Canadian Express Company should refuse to carry all consignments of booze—except as above at the direction of the relief committee.

It should at once be declared a criminal offence to transport liquor in Halifax, or this province, while the present chaotic state continues.

This terrible menace must be quickly crushed. The military and naval authorities should co-operate to the utmost of their powers to prevent the incoming of booze, which would intensify the terrible nature of the tragedy which has befallen the city.

A prominent official of the U.S.A. naval forces, attached to one of the U.S. ships now in the harbor, and who was an officer in connection with the first relief ship that entered San Francisco after the great earthquake which laid that city in ruins, was interviewed by the *Halifax Herald*. This officer stated that martial law was immediately enforced and armed soldiers were stationed at regular intervals along the streets. A patrol merely walking the streets is not so effective as men stationed on short beats; crooks and toughs simply wait till the passing of the patrol; but with the streets sectioned off into short beats the protection is obviously more complete. TWENTY CIVILIANS WERE SHOT IN THE FIRST TWO HOURS for attempting to loot bodies and raid empty houses. "'Blind Pigs' or 'Blind Tigers' as we call them," said this officer, "received SWIFT treatment. Just as a concrete example of how we handled the 'booze' situation in 'Frisco after the earthquake," he went on, "is the following:

"We located a dive, and a lieutenant of the regular army with two squads of sixteen men, armed with shoulder rifles, formed up before the building. The lieutenant walked into the dive and ordered the immediate dispersion of the inmates. Four left out of eighteen. The lieutenant waved his hand and the squads fired one round into the air; several more of the joint inmates then left the premises, a second command was given and SEVEN WHO REFUSED TO LEAVE THE DIVE WERE INSTANTLY SHOT. It was all over in less than fifteen minutes. We had no more trouble with 'booze' or 'bootleggers'," said the officer.

WE ARE FACING THE SAME DANGER IN HALIFAX. We must have ACTION! The present conditions in this city demand that action quick.

153

Potter's Field on Bayers Road was the site of a mass grave for the unidentified dead. Here, local Boy Scouts take part in a ceremony marking the monument.

In the howling gales that followed closely on the day of disaster, the *Picton,* with her cargo of shells, dragged her anchor around the harbour, so she was boarded and beached.

In the days that followed, a number of people reported seeing smoke issuing from the ship, and when the newspapers published stories to this effect, insistent demands were made by an excusably overwrought populace that she be taken to sea and scuttled.

The reiterated assurances of experts that there was no danger of a second explosion failed to still the clamour, and on December 10 things came to a head.

Early on the morning of that day, two soldiers of the 63rd Regiment, doing guard duty on shore, saw a blaze of light on board the *Picton,* followed by a mass of smoke. When they saw a number of men leaving the ship in panic, the soldiers were in no doubt that they were witnessing the beginning of a second disaster, and fled, shouting a warning to everyone they met.

154

When the civic authorities hastily contacted the captain superintendent of the dockyard, their demand for immediate action could not, he felt, be ignored, and reluctantly he gave orders for the ship to be hauled off and scuttled.

FROM: Senior Naval Officer (British) Halifax, N.S.
TO: Commander in Chief, N.A. & W.I., H.M.S. *Leviathan.*
DATE: 13 December, 1917.

On Monday, 10 December, I received a report that S.S. *Picton,* containing ammunition was on fire and that she was being taken out of harbour to be sunk.

Further enquiry resulted in the discovery that her decks were littered with some chemical believed to be a residue of the explosion which was intermittently bursting into flames, also I was informed that the papers were full of scare paragraphs on the subject, and that it was desirable to quiet public opinion. Feeling sure that no such action was necessary and that this fine ship must be preserved, I entered a protest against such a drastic remedy and went afloat to investigate the matter myself.

I found Captain Newton, R.N., of the *Calgarian* already on the spot and preparing to anchor the ship. He stated that the mysterious chemical was really the phosphorus from her smoke producing apparatus, small pieces of this material had been scattered about her decks by the explosion, and had been ignited several times by the feet of men going on board her from the Canadian Patrols. It seems that on the last occasion a rather larger mass than usual had become ignited and those on the spot had become panic stricken and left the ship.

Captain Newton had intercepted a signal from the Canadian *P.V.4,* "Steamship *Picton* on fire am leaving east passage." Knowing that the *Picton* contained ammunition Captain Newton very gallantly proceeded to the spot and boarded her, throwing overboard the phosphorus which remained on her deck. Though the risk of explosion was not great, owing to the ammunition being boxed in the lower hold, whilst the fire was on deck and not likely to spread, he could not know this until he had made his investigation.

Several orders came, whilst I was on board, to sink the *Picton* but, in view of the circumstances, I negatived them and the ship was anchored. Owing to the anchors having been slipped when moving her down the harbour, only one anchor and forty fathoms cable remained but she was in a safe position and would come to no harm even if tailing ashore. I have approached her agents with a view to getting the cargo shifted to some other vessel. The *Picton* is in a state which renders it impossible that she can be got ready for sea for some time. Her stern post is broken, decks swept and masses of stone, many tons in weight have wrecked the deck cabins and are now lying where they have fallen.

In the face of public fury and indignation, Chambers, with the full support of the commander in chief and the admiralty, continued to refuse all demands that the *Picton* be scuttled, and there was no second explosion.

Eventually the ship was unloaded, repaired, and then taken to sea again.

Rear Admiral Chambers, in a later report, gave news of the convoy that had been due to sail on December 7.

The slow convoy left with a total of thirty-three vessels. The delay has been considerable but the *Highflyer* was only ready on Loth and the weather was so bad that had the convoy left on Saturday, it would have been hove to and possibly scattered.

I motored along Barrington Street today which, from King Edward Hotel north to Africville, is wrecked either by the explosion or the resulting fire.

We passed various parties with maps, mapping the ruined areas and were able to see that many bodies are still being recovered though the deep snow and terrible confusion into which this area has been thrown, must make the work very difficult.

Passing down the hill to my office, I observed that the whole of Argyle Street, above the esplanade, was full of what I first took to be packing crates, then I realised they were rough coffins.

On Monday, December 17, the two hundred still-unclaimed dead were gathered in rows of coffins outside the Chebucto Road School. In the presence of a large, silent crowd, clergy of all denominations held a mass funeral service. Then the coffins were loaded on a convoy of open motor trucks, and slowly the cortège, headed by the cars carrying the clergymen, wound its way out toward the Fairview Cemetery. At the gate of the cemetery the procession was waved down imperiously by an official.

When the officer in charge of the funeral detail demanded an explanation, he was told that there had been a mistake. As the dead were unidentified, and therefore without estates or relatives to meet the cost of burial plots, it had been decided that Fairview could not accept them. The official said that alternative arrangements had been made, and that a mass grave had been dug on a piece of unconsecrated waste ground in Bayers Road.

With great difficulty, the cortège turned in the narrow driveway, and the dead with no names were carried to their last resting place in Halifax's Potter's Field.

CHAPTER NINE
"I HAVE A WARRANT FOR YOUR ARREST"

Long before the stubbornest of the fires in Richmond had been put out, or the mortuaries had received the last excavated corpse, the people of Halifax were clamouring for an investigation into the disaster. Their vociferous demand was that the authorities act at once, and that no effort be spared, no susceptibilities considered, in their determination to fix responsibility. The slogan "Place the Blame" rapidly developed into an hysterical cry for vengeance.

There was little doubt in the minds of most citizens that the real culprit was, of course, the kaiser. It was he, after all, who had started the war, and if he had not, then the *Mont Blanc* would never have put into Halifax with so deadly a cargo. Unfortunately, though, hanging him for his crime was out of the question while the Imperial armies held their ground on every battlefront. But there were others of the same nationality closer at hand, the few Germans who had their homes in Halifax.

Hitherto, they had been allowed their liberty and required to report only once a month. Now the full fury of the Haligonians' wrath was turned upon them. Men, women, and children with names like Richter or Schultz were stoned in the streets, or chased by angry crowds that were largely made up of people who, only a week earlier, had been friendly neighbours.

A story was circulated that, on Young Avenue, a Herr Hobrecker had a concrete gun emplacement under his lawn for the use of an invading army. The rumour also had it that on the morning of the disaster his maid was seen opening all the windows in the house long before the explosion, in anticipation of the blast.

The wild mob that rushed to the address to expose the "spy" found that the Hobrecker home had been slightly damaged, and that the family had left. Disappointed at losing their prey, they tore the house apart, and then went away satisfied that in some small way justice had been done.

Similar incidents were reported elsewhere, and throughout the city, the people were in an ugly mood. On December 10, acting upon the instructions of the military, the chief of police arrested every German citizen.

Anyone who may have questioned the necessity for these wholesale arrests, or who doubted the emperor's guilt for the tragedy with the connivance and complicity of his subjects in the town, had only to read the newspapers to be reassured. In a leading article on December 12, the *Halifax Herald* added its voice to the "Hate the Hometown Hun" campaign:

...WE NOW KNOW, TOO, THAT THE PRIME RESPONSIBILITY for this, as for every other catastrophe which has afflicted the peoples of the earth as a by-product of the war, rests with that close co-partner, that arch fiend, the Emperor of the Germans; neither are we disposed to hold the German peoples entirely free of direct responsibility for this catastrophe; the cause is obscure; but IT IS CERTAIN THAT THERE ARE IN HALIFAX TODAY CERTAIN PEOPLE OF GERMAN EXTRACTION AND BIRTH whose citizenship in the Dominion has been respected since the war began, who have been allowed full freedom in our community to buy and sell, and to pursue their normal occupations, WHO HAVE REPAID US WITHIN THE PAST FEW DAYS BY LAUGHING OPENLY AT OUR DISTRESS AND MOCKING OUR SORROW.

"There are strange things afoot. There are rumours, which may indeed be no more than rumours, of a ship suddenly sunken in the harbour for possibly dark design, and of signals from house-tops at night, which are not calculated to make easier the sad hearts of the survivors of this disaster. So long as there are people in Halifax who remember this past week, or whose children remember it, so long will the name of German be a name for loathing and disgust. This if for no other reason, because we know NOW, what war is. And Germany, alone among all the Nations of the earth, makes war with DELIBERATE INTENT.

But the turning of jail keys on a score of Meyersteins, Bauermanns, and Schmidts failed to be satisfactory even as a gesture, and before long even the most gullible Haligonian began to realize the impossibility of the explosion having been the result of some deep laid German plot. Who, then, was responsible? The *Mont Blanc?* The *Imo?* The navy?

On December 13, after one or two postponements, an investigation before the wreck commissioners opened in the old court house on Spring Garden Road, for the express purpose of apportioning the blame.

The chairman of the commission was the local judge in admiralty, the Honourable Arthur Drysdale, justice of the Supreme Court of Canada, assisted by Captain Demers, FRAS, FRSA, and Captain Hose, RCN, captain of patrols, acting as nautical assessors.

W. A. Henry, KC, appeared on behalf of the Dominion

government, and Humphrey Mellish, KC, and Joseph P. Nolan, a lawyer from New York who was granted all the privileges of the Bar, represented the owners of the *Mont Blanc.*

Appearing on behalf of the *Imo*'s owners was a local counsel of almost legendary repute: C. J. Burchell, KC, F. H. Bell, KC, A. Cluney, KC, and T. R. Robertson, KC, had been briefed by the city of Halifax, the attorney general of Nova Scotia, and the Halifax Pilotage Commission, respectively.

Before the hearing began, which was to last, with one very long adjournment, until January 28, 1918, Mr. Henry rose to make an appeal that any witness to the collision unknown to the court should come forward. Louis D'Ornano, technical translator of the Department of Marine, Ottawa, was then sworn in as an interpreter, and Captain Aimé Le Medec took the stand.

Through the interpreter, Le Medec testified to his training and experience before being assigned to the *Mont Blanc,* and detailed the loading of the ship at Gravesend Bay, New York. He then went on to explain the reason for his voyage to Halifax, and told of the instructions he received from the examining officer at the mouth of the harbour when he arrived.

Questioned by Mr. Henry, he stated that when the *Mont Blanc* passed the *Highflyer* she was approximately 150 metres from the Dartmouth shore, that she remained in her rightful waters throughout, and that when the *Imo* was first seen, her starboard side was visible to those on the French ship. She seemed to be cutting across the *Mont Blanc*'s course, bearing two to two-and-a-half points from the port bow. Le Medec then went into considerable detail concerning the manoeuvring of his ship and the whistle signals that had been given.

When the captain had described the collision, Mr. Henry asked him, "What happened then?"

"When I saw the flames add themselves to the smoke, I thought that the ship was to be blown up at once. It was impossible to do anything at all to stop the fire, and in order not to sacrifice uselessly the lives of forty men, I gave the order to lower the boats and get into them."

Questioned further on the evacuation of the ship, Le Medec denied that there was any panic at all on board, and said that his order was executed very quickly and with the greatest calm on the part of the crew. He also told the court that, with the exception of the gunner Yves Gueguiner, who had since died of the wounds he had received, none of his crew was severely injured in the explosion.

In a little while it was Burchell's turn to cross-examine.

The counsel for the Norwegian shipping company had the disadvantage of not being able to call as witnesses for the case of the *Imo* either the captain or the pilot, as they had both been killed. In fact, only one officer from the ship was available to testify, which left the counsel with no alternative but to attempt to break down the stories of the men of the *Mont Blanc,* or any other witness whose testimony seemed to be in their favour. He was to prove, throughout the inquiry, capable of the most ruthless courtroom tactics, and was constantly to attack and browbeat witnesses. He was more than aided in the course he had chosen to adopt by the judge, who from early on showed a bias in favour of the *Imo.*

Le Medec and his crew also had one great disadvantage—the fact that they were Frenchmen, which, in the eyes of the majority of Nova Scotians, made them capable of almost anything.

The strong anti-French feeling, evident not only in the Maritime provinces but in many other parts of Canada, stemmed from a fierce political conflict that had developed earlier in the war.

In 1914, the status of Canada was that of a self-governing colony rather than an independent state. She was accordingly committed to the British government's declaration of war on Germany, but although she could not have stayed neutral, it was for her own government to decide the extent of her participation in the struggle.

In the main, the Canadian people rallied to aid Britain, and in the beginning there were many volunteers for the services; but by 1916, voluntary enlistment was falling off, and Sir Robert Borden's government was obliged to think in terms of compulsion.

After a bitter contest in parliament, the Military Service Act became law on August 29, 1917; but the conscription policy was unpopular in many areas of Canada, and above all in the province of Quebec, where the fiercely nationalistic French-speaking Canadians, the majority of whom were opposed to their country becoming involved in any way in the European conflict, demanded that the Act be revoked, or at least amended to exclude them.

This attitude on their part did not endear them to their fellow countrymen, and when later there was serious and extensive rioting in Quebec over the conscription issue, the country was split wide open.

The words "French Canadian" became to some people almost synonymous with traitor, and to these people's muddled way of thinking, the attitude of Quebec must surely be the attitude of France.

To the citizens of Halifax, the fact that the ship that had destroyed their city was flying the tricolour had been the final blow, and had greatly increased their understandable hostility toward the crew. In many homes, the case had been pre-judged, and the *Mont Blanc* found guilty.

Burchell went into the attack at once and, questioning the French captain closely, tried on several occasions to break him down, particularly in regard to the sequence of the whistle signals; but Le Medec remained calm and merely repeated what he had said earlier.

Throughout examination and cross-examination, the captain constantly clasped and unclasped his hands, and from time to time nervously rolled his handkerchief into a hard pad. Nonetheless, the reporter from the *Halifax Herald* noted "...to all questions he gave direct answers, his eyes never leaving the questioner."

Burchell then put the question that was uppermost in the minds of many. "Did your ship carry any red flag, or anything to indicate that she was loaded with munitions?"

Le Medec shook his head. "No, sir," he replied, through D'Ornano.

"Why not?"

"Because the red flag, according to international regulations, indicates that explosives are being handled on board ship, that it is in process of loading or discharging munitions. Nowhere do the regulations say that it must be flown when a ship is under way, and I was of the opinion that, particularly at this time, it was preferable that everyone should be in ignorance of the nature of my cargo."

When he was asked whether or not he spoke English, Le Medec hesitated for a moment, and then answered, "Only a very little." He agreed that the pilot, Mackey, could not speak any French, but denied that this made for any lack of understanding between them on the bridge. "We spoke mostly in signs," he said, "and everything was clear between us."

Later in the inquiry, however, when the captain was recalled to the witness stand, he was to admit that in fact he spoke English quite well, having had to learn it for his Master's Certificate, but he said that he did not like to use it because sometimes people seemed not to understand him.

As the days passed, a succession of witnesses took the stand, and among them were the second officer of the *Imo* and several members of her crew. Between them, and again testifying through an interpreter, they gave evidence about their ship and her movements on the fatal day.

For the most part, their testimony confirmed the case put forward by the ship's owners, which was that the *Imo,* originally the White Star liner *Runic* built in 1889, was proceeding in ballast to sea from Bedford Basin bound for New York, under a charter between her owners, the South Pacific Whaling Company and the Belgian Relief Commission. The weather was clear generally, but there was a slight haze in the upper part of the Narrows.

The Norwegian vessel left her anchorage on the western shore of the Basin, on the morning of the collision, shortly after eight o'clock, in charge of a duly licensed pilot, William Hayes.

As she was about to enter the Narrows at a speed which all the witnesses who were on board insisted was not greater than 5 knots, an American tramp steamer was coming up against the Halifax shore, which was, for her, the wrong side of the channel, and the *Imo,* to avoid a collision, was forced over into Dartmouth waters.

The pilot of the American ship, Edward Renner, in his evidence was later to challenge this statement, and said that he was holding a course in mid-channel at the time.

The witnesses from the relief ship then asserted that before the *Imo* could correct her position, the *Stella Maris* was sighted with her barges. The tug was heading across their bows toward the Dartmouth shore but suddenly turned back, so that, had the Norwegian altered course then, she would have rammed the smaller vessel. Thus, she was forced to continue down against the Dartmouth shore.

When the *Imo* blew a one-blast signal to the *Mont Blanc,* which had previously been seen at a considerable distance, it was alleged that the French ship was not keeping in close to the Dartmouth shore at all, but was working out to mid-channel, angling across to the Halifax side and cutting across the course of the Norwegian.

Abreast of the *Stella Maris,* off Pier 9, the *Imo* blew a three-blast signal and reversed her engines. The distance between her and the *Mont Blanc* at this time was from one-half to three-quarters of a mile.

With the engines reversed, the bow of the *Imo* swung to starboard, toward the Halifax side, and from that moment until the time of the collision, she was never heading towards the Dartmouth shore, but in the opposite direction, under a steady helm.

After the engines were reversed, they were stopped, and remained so until just before the collision. The next signal was one blast from the *Mont Blanc,* said by some of the witnesses to have been quickly repeated. The *Imo* replied to this with a single blast, and continued turning to starboard in accordance with her signal.

The *Mont Blanc* by then, according to the South Pacific Whaling Company's case, had worked pretty well out to mid-channel, but the two ships were then in their respective waters, and could, and should, have passed safely port to port. It was stated that the *Mont Blanc* then blew a cross signal of two blasts and swung to port on a starboard helm, throwing herself across the channel in front of the bows of the *Imo,* making a collision inevitable.

The relief ship immediately blew a three-blast signal and reversed her engines full speed astern, but it was too late, and she struck the *Mont Blanc* a glancing blow.

It was hardly surprising that on nearly every point concerning the signals and manoeuvres of the two ships, the witnesses from the *Mont Blanc* and the *Imo* disagreed, and there was a considerable amount of confusing testimony given in regard to the signals by independent witnesses.

Further evidence of the spy and saboteur hysteria that had seized the city after the explosion was brought to light during the inquiry, and concerned one of the witnesses from the *Imo*. Burchell revealed that, some days earlier, he had visited the survivors of the Norwegian ship who were then being held on board *Highflyer*. He found that one of them, Johan Johansen, who had been at the helm of the *Imo* at the time of the collision and was, therefore, a vital witness, was confined to the sick bay with injuries.

After conferring with the counsel for the Dominion government, Burchell arranged for this man to be taken ashore, and in due course, Johansen was transferred to Bellevue Hospital. When, however, Burchell arrived at the hospital the following evening to interview him, he was told that the Norwegian had been removed to the city prison and that he was being held there, under armed guard, in a cell.

Furious at not having been consulted, the KC demanded an explanation, and he was told by the military authorities that it had been reported to them by a nurse at the hospital that the young sailor had acted in a "suspicious manner." According to their informant, he had been caught trying to leave the hospital and had been sent back to his ward by the medical officer. Later in the evening, he had offered twenty-five dollars to one of the volunteer nurses if she would allow him to go home, and then had asked for a newspaper. These facts, on being reported to the officer in charge of the hospital, had been enough to make him suspect that he was dealing with a dangerous German spy, and when he searched the sailor's belongings and found among them a letter written in Norwegian, which he took to be German, he was convinced, and sent for the provost marshal.

Eventually, after several days spent in argument with military intelligence, Burchell secured Johansen's release. It was then that the bewildered seaman explained that the only reason he had attempted to leave the hospital was because the doctors there had refused to take his injuries seriously and had not given him any treatment. This despite the fact that a local physician who had examined him earlier had found him suffering from a severe cut on the leg and badly lacerated eyes.

It was on the second day of the inquiry that Francis Mackey took the oath. Under examination by Mr. Mellish and Mr. Henry, he confirmed Le Medec's account of the actions taken by the *Mont Blanc* and the sequence of the signals given by her. Then he went on to tell of how the ship was abandoned, and of sighting Lieutenant Commander Murray when in the lifeboat, and of his attempts to warn him.

When Henry, to squash an ugly rumour that had been circulated, asked him, "Tell me, pilot, for your own sake, whether you had been drinking any liquor that day?"

Mackey replied, "None whatever."

"You had none on board the French ship the night before?"

"None."

"And when you started to take the French ship in the next morning, you were perfectly sober?"

"Yes, sir," replied the pilot in a clear voice.

When, two days later, Mackey was recalled to the stand, he was to face a bitter cross-examination from Burchell, whose obvious intention was to discredit the pilot in every possible way.

Rising slowly, the counsel for the *Imo* opened his attack with some seemingly routine questions concerning the movement of the two ships; then he asked, "Did you see the *Stella Maris* drop her barges and go back to try and put your fire out?"

Mackey shook his head. "I did not notice."

Burchell pressed the point further. "Do you know, as a matter of fact, that the *Stella Maris* did go alongside, and that the captain and officers performed a great deed of heroism in trying to put this fire out?"

"I heard that."

"Did you not notice her drop her barges?"

"No, sir."

"Never noticed her anchor her barges and turn back?"

"No, all my attention was taken up with the boats."

Without attempting to disguise the sneer in his voice, Burchell struck out with, "All your attention was taken up in saving your life." Then, later, having dealt with the collision and the steps Mackey had taken to warn anyone in the immediate vicinity, he culminated his cross-examination with a savage personal attack. Quietly he asked, "You know, of course, that many people were killed in the explosion that followed?"

"Yes."

"Do you know that there were some thousands severely wounded and injured for life?"

"Yes."

"And do you know that 2:30 today is the hour set for the funeral of a large number of unidentified victims of the explosion?"

Mackey shook his head. "I didn't know that."

"Did you know that the bells ringing now are for this funeral?"

Again the pilot shook his head. "No, I have not heard them."

"I want to ask you now, knowing that this is the hour for the funeral, if you are willing to admit frankly that you have been deliberately perjuring yourself for the last two days?"

"No."

"You say that everything you told us is absolutely true?"

"To the best of my knowledge; to the best of my ability."

"You say that at this hour?"

"Yes."

Burchell leaned forward and repeated the question slowly, his voice ringing through the hushed courtroom. "You say that at this hour?"

Without hesitation, Mackey replied, "Yes."

There was a long pause, and then counsel went on, "You are a considerably hard drinker?"

"No."

"Sometimes you get drunk?"

"Not lately. I have sometimes, a long while ago."

"You drink quite a bit, though, eh? What is known as a constant drinker?" Now Burchell had adopted a friendly, almost confidential tone, as though he were trying to get the pilot to share a secret with him which he would keep to himself, but Mackey was not taken in.

"No, not a heavy drinker," he replied.

Mackey's sobriety was confirmed when James Hall, sheriff of the County of Halifax and chairman of the Pilotage Commission, took the stand. He said that he had known him for thirty years, and that he considered Mackey to be one of the best pilots in the harbour; sober, industrious, and attentive to his duties. Never had the commissioners had any reason to complain about his habits, nor had he, personally, ever seen Mackey under the influence of liquor or heard it reported.

As Hall was about to leave the stand, he was called back by Captain Demers, who asked him, "Is Pilot Mackey allowed to pilot at the present moment?"

Hall appeared somewhat surprised at the question. "Why, yes sir," he replied.

"Is it right that whilst Pilot Mackey is under examination, and pending the findings of the court, that he should be exercising his duties as a pilot?"

"Pending the decision of the investigation, the Pilotage Commission have not seen their way clear to interfere," was the chairman's somewhat indignant answer.

Demers shook his head in amazement. "They have not suspended him from his functions, not even for the time being?"

The Halifax Explosion Memorial Bell Tower at Fort Needham Memorial Park near the Hydrostone section in the city's North End.

"No, sir, they have not."

On recall, Hall was again questioned as to why Mackey had not been suspended. He was forced to admit that this was largely due to the fact that there were so few pilots available. When pressed on this point, he conceded that, owing to the great shortage, the few men who were licensed were compelled to work very long hours.

During the closing stages of the inquiry, Captain Pasco and Commander Frederick Wyatt, the chief examining officer, were called to give their evidence.

171

Having described his actions on the day of the explosion, Pasco, his wounded head still partly covered with bandages, was asked by Mr. Henry for his definition of the regulations concerning a ship flying the red explosives flag. The captain replied that, as far as he understood it, such a signal meant the whole world over that a ship was working munitions either out of or into her holds, and that when this operation was completed and the holds closed, the flag was lowered.

"What would you say, in view of war conditions, as to the advisability of a ship flying the red flag approaching or leaving a port?"

There was no doubt in Pasco's mind as to the proper answer to this. "It would be suicidal. Giving information to enemy agents."

Questioned further as to who could have stopped the *Imo* leaving anchorage, Pasco replied that only the chief examining officer had such authority. The pilots had orders that they were not to lift anchor unless they had permission from Wyatt, and as Pasco understood it, the *Imo* had not been given permission to leave that morning.

This matter-of-fact statement caused a sensation in the courtroom, as it confirmed one of the many rumours then circulating.

Pasco concluded his evidence by saying that the thing that surprised him most about the whole sad affair was that the *Mont Blanc* had ever been loaded with such a combination of explosives. "I cannot understand," he said, "why her crew did not protest when they were in New York, and leave the ship in a body."

Commander Frederick Evans Wyatt followed Pasco into the witness box. He testified that, as chief examining officer, the movements of all large vessels in the harbour were under his authority. He was responsible for saying where merchant ships should berth, and when they should enter or leave the port. He agreed, when it was put to him, that he had been notified of the cargo of the *Mont Blanc* by Lieutenant Freeman at about 5:30 P.M. on December 5.

Asked about the *Imo,* he said that he had had no idea that she was ready for sea that morning, but this was not unusual, for, despite the fact that he had written to all shipping agents and pilots some time previously asking them to inform him of any proposed sailings, this was very often not done.

"Was it not the duty of the guard-ship to intercept this vessel ship?"

"No, sir. The duties of the guard-ship are merely to examine and guard suspect neutral vessels using the harbour. It is not concerned in any way with Allied shipping."

Mr. Bell then put the question, "As far as you knew, there was no risk of any collision that morning?"

"None whatever."

"Because you believed there was no ship going out?"

"Yes."

"Had the tragedy not occurred, what would have happened to the *Imo?*"

"I should have tried to stop her by firing a shot across her bows, either from one of the patrol vessels or from the forts."

"Have you had any other instances of ships going out without permission?"

"I had one happen two days ago."

"Before the collision, had you had any instances?"

"The pilots have not been in the habit of carrying out my instructions as they should. There were one or two instances, which I reported to my superior officer, Captain Martin, the captain superintendent, and in each case the ship was shot at and stopped."

"Were the pilots in question punished?"

"No, sir. There has never seemed to be any way of punishing pilots for violations of this kind."

When cross-examining, Burchell suggested that if the guard-ship had been requested to do so, she could have informed Wyatt of any ships leaving the harbour without authority, and in that way he would have had absolute control over all movements. The chief examining officer agreed that this was true, but said that he preferred to work through the pilots personally, and that as things stood, it was up to them to inform him.

Counsel then said that he had been instructed by the clerk in the pilot's office that for several weeks he had carefully advised Wyatt each day of steamers that were about to move. The clerk, a sixteen-year-old boy, would testify, when he was called, that often he telephoned with a list of fifteen or sixteen ships, and that on these occasions he always spoke to the chief examining officer. However, after some time he was convinced that Wyatt was not taking the names down and seemed to be laughing at him. Burchell asked the naval officer if this was so.

The commander agreed that the clerk seemed to have got some peculiar idea like this into his head, but said that it was ridiculous. He admitted, though, that when the boy stopped telephoning information concerning sailings, he had not bothered to take the matter up with anyone.

Later, in a heated exchange, Burchell suggested that Wyatt could have done more to ensure the co-operation of the pilots. He said also that it was obvious that, in doing nothing more than reporting these occasional violations by the pilots to his superior officer, he was trying to shift responsibility for his own laxity.

Before the commander could reply, Mr. Henry jumped to his feet. "My Lord, I object to counsel speaking of shifting responsibility; it is high time I said something. My learned friend from the first, with regard to the evidence of any witness which did not suit him, has persistently abused and used language in regard to these witnesses which I do not think should have been allowed. I have no personal interest whatsoever in the result of this inquiry, but my learned friend should be restrained from asking questions involving criticism of others."

Somewhat grudgingly, justice Drysdale agreed, and mildly admonished Burchell.

The counsel for the *Imo* then went on to question Commander Wyatt on conditions in the dockyard following the disaster. "Tell me," he said, "do you know anything about the threatened second explosion?"

"No, I don't. I understand, and I feel almost sure, that it was a scare started by the military owing to the fire having come close to the magazine."

"On the morning of the explosion, I was personally engaged in rescue work, and I met a person, a sailor, who said he had been warned out of the dockyard by you because you said there was a danger of a second explosion," Burchell announced.

"Would you mind giving me his name?"

"I will give it later on."

Wyatt was rapidly becoming extremely annoyed at this line of questioning. "I must have his name in open court," he insisted, but Burchell continued as if he had not heard him. "Was there an alarm in the dockyard about that second explosion?" he asked.

"My first business, after putting a few dead bodies on a cart, was to get to my office. As to telling anybody to leave the dockyard, I never spoke to anyone after the explosion, and if you will give me the name of the man, I will take the necessary action."

Counsel made a mock attempt at calming the ruffled witness. "I am not insinuating anything. I just want to know if there was any danger of a second explosion, because that was the report I got." But Wyatt was not to be put off that easily.

"If there had been a strong northerly wind, the fire might well have got to the magazine before the ammunition had been shifted. But I want to get the name of the man who said I ordered him out."

"Suggested," corrected Burchell.

"I want to know who it was."

It was the learned counsel's turn now to be on the defensive. "There's nothing wrong," he said hastily.

"I would not even have *suggested* that any man leave the dockyard when everybody there was needed."

"But was a general alarm given to clear out of the dockyard?"

"No, that is certainly not true."

"Would you be surprised to learn that I saw at least forty sailors from the *Niobe* in town?" asked counsel.

"There were hundreds of us up there fighting the fire. There may well have been isolated cases of men running to their homes to see to their families, but as to saying there was a stampede in the dockyard, that is rot."

"There was considerable commotion because of the fear of a second explosion?" Burchell suggested.

"I did not notice it in the half-hour I was there."

"The question I asked you was whether anyone had been told, sailors or anyone else, to leave the dockyard because there was danger?"

"No such order was given, to my certain knowledge."

"Well, if that is correct, the statements given to me cannot be correct." Burchell was smiling blandly now. "It was a sailor who came down and was with me on relief work. He mentioned your name in connection with it, but of course, if it is incorrect..."

"It is up to you to let me have that man's name, and I will deal with him on his ship," demanded Wyatt.

Captain Demers interrupted here to support the chief

examining officer. "I think he should have the name," he said, and he looked to justice Drysdale for a ruling. His Lordship nodded, and directed Burchell, "Give him the name of the person."

The counsel appeared flustered. "It was a sailor on rescue work with me," he said. " Actually, two people told me."

"In that case," countered Wyatt, "I should have both names."

"Mr. Burchell," instructed the judge, "if anyone told you that Commander Wyatt gave an order that the dockyard was to be evacuated, then give him the names of the people concerned."

Again Burchell prevaricated. "Well, as I understood it, there was an order for everyone to leave the dockyard, as there was a danger of a second explosion, and Commander Wyatt's name was mentioned in connection with this order."

"But he denies it," the judge reminded him.

"Absolutely." Wyatt was having great difficulty in controlling himself. "I did not speak to anyone in the dockyard after the explosion. In an open court, and during an investigation like this, there is a certain charge being made against me by an unknown sailor, suggesting that I ordered people out of the dockyard, and it is cowardly."

There was no doubt now in Burchell's mind that he had gone too far, and he hastened to pour oil on the troubled waters. "Oh, but it was not a man working. It was, after all, quite proper for him to leave the dockyard."

Still Wyatt would not be put off. "No, we had need of every man there."

Slowly Mr. Henry got to his feet. "As I understand it, Your Lordship has directed that my learned friend should give, in open court, the names of the two people who have made this charge. Is that not so?"

"Yes," replied Drysdale. "I think in fairness he ought to do that."

"Well, a nurse from the hospital, a Miss Barnstead, was one who told me, the other was a sailor. I don't know his name."

With Burchell's admission, Wyatt relaxed a little, but not before he had snapped, "Then you should not have brought it up, that is hearsay evidence."

During the course of his evidence, Wyatt was asked whether he thought it was dangerous at all for two ships to pass in the Narrows.

"Certainly not," he replied. "The *Olympic,* sister ship to the *Titanic,* has passed the *Mauretania* many times in the Narrows quite safely, and there are no ships bigger than these."

On January 28, 1918, all the available witnesses having been examined, the hearing ended, and on February 4, Mr. Justice Drysdale made public his findings. His report caused a tremendous sensation in Halifax, and was the subject of grave discussions in merchant shipping circles and in the offices of the admiralty on Whitehall.

HALIFAX, N.S.
4 February, 1918

Sir,

Having been directed by the Honourable the Minister of Marine to hold a formal enquiry into the cause of the explosion on the s.s. *Mont Blanc* on 6 December, 1917, I have to report as follows:

That as directed I had associated with me as Nautical Assessors, Captain Demers of Ottawa, Dominion Wreck Commissioner, and Captain Walter Hose, R.C.N. of the City of Halifax. I began the enquiry on the 13th day of December, A.D. 1917, and having heard all the witnesses that could throw any light on the situation, and having conferred with the Nautical Assessors, I have reached the following conclusions and desire to report as follows:

1. The explosion on the s.s. *Mont Blanc* on 6 December was entirely the result of a collision in the harbour between s.s. *Mont Blanc* and the s.s. *Imo*.

2. Such collision was caused by violation of the rules of Navigation.

3. That the Pilot and Master of the s.s. *Mont Blanc* were wholly responsible for violating the rules of the road.

4. That Pilot Mackey by reason of his gross negligence should be forthwith dismissed by the Pilotage Authorities and his licence cancelled.

5. In view of the gross neglect of the rules of Navigation by Pilot Mackey, the attention of the Law Officers of the Crown should be called to the evidence taken at this investigation with a view to a criminal prosecution of such pilot.

6. We recommend to the French Authorities such evidence with a view to having Captain Le Medec's licence cancelled and such captain dealt with according to the law of his country.

7. That it appearing that the Pilotage Authorities in Halifax have been permitting Pilot Mackey to pilot ships since the investigation commenced and since the collision above referred to, we think the Authorities, i.e. Pilotage Authorities, deserving of censure. In our opinion the Authorities should have promptly suspended such pilot.

8. The Master and Pilot of the *Mont Blanc* are guilty of neglect of the public safety in not taking proper steps to warn the inhabitants of the city of a probable explosion.

9. Commander Wyatt is guilty of neglect in performing his duty as C.X.O. in not taking proper steps to ensure the regulations being carried out and especially in not keeping himself fully acquainted with the movements and intended movements of vessels in the harbour.

10. In dealing with the C.X.O.'s negligence in not ensuring the efficient carrying out of traffic regulations by the pilots we have to

report that the evidence is far from satisfactory that he ever took any efficient steps to bring to the notice of the Captain Superintendent neglect on the part of the pilots.

11. In view of the allegations of disobedience of the C.X.O.'s orders by pilots, we do not consider such disobedience was the proximate cause of the collision.

12. It would seem that the pilots of Halifax attempt to vary the well known Rules of the Road, and, in this connection, we think Pilot Renner, in charge of an American tramp steamer on the morning of the collision, deserving of censure.

13. The regulations governing the traffic in Halifax Harbour in force since the war were prepared by the competent Naval Authorities; that such traffic regulations do not satisfactorily deal with the handling of ships laden with explosives and we have to recommend that such competent Authority forthwith take up and make satisfactory regulations dealing with such subject; we realise that whilst war goes on under present conditions explosives must move but, in view of what has happened, we strongly recommend that the subject be dealt with satisfactorily by the proper Authorities.

Given under my hand at the City of Halifax this Fourth day of February, 1918.

Immediately after the reading of Drysdale's findings, warrants were issued at the instance of the Attorney General's Department for the arrest of Captain Le Medec, Pilot Mackey, and Commander Frederick Wyatt, on a charge of manslaughter.

With William Hayes, the pilot of the *Imo,* named as the specific victim, the warrants set forth that, "Francis Mackey of Halifax, pilot; Aimé Le Medec at present of Halifax, sea captain; Frederick Evans Wyatt at present of Halifax, Commander, R.N.R., did at Halifax aforesaid on the Sixth day of December, A.D. Nineteen Hundred and Seventeen, unlawfully kill and slay one

William Hayes, as this deponent is informed and doth verily believe and hath good grounds for so believing."

Mackey and Wyatt were taken into custody almost immediately, and half an hour later, Chief of Police Hanrahan walked up to Le Medec on the corner of Prince and Granville Streets and, stepping in front of him, said, "I have a warrant for your arrest."

All three men were released again immediately on very heavy bail being posted, and within a few days they appeared for a preliminary hearing before Stipendiary McLeod, who committed them for trial before the Supreme Court.

The charge of manslaughter against Aimé Le Medec, and Drysdale's recommendation that the French government should strip him of his license, were the immediate concern of the Fédération des Syndicats de Capitaines au Long Cours de France who, on March 11, 1918, wrote to the minister of marine in Paris on the captain's behalf.

LE HARVE, *le 11 mars, 1918*

Monsieur le Ministre,

We have the honour to appeal for your kind attention to Master Mariner Le Medec, ex-Commandant of the steamship *Mont Blanc.*

The *Mont Blanc,* following a collision with another steamship, blew up in the roads of Halifax and the explosion destroyed a quarter of the town. There were a number of dead and wounded and a part of the population found themselves for several days without shelter, a situation made very distressing by a violent snowstorm accompanied by a most low temperature.

The catastrophe was caused by a wrong manoeuvre of the steamship on opposite tack which collided with the *Mont Blanc,* full of explosives and petrol.

181

Some time ago a press dispatch advised us that the Canadian pilot responsible for bringing in the *Mont Blanc* had been dismissed, that Captain Le Medec had been blamed and that the Canadian Authorities were demanding that the French Government withdraw his Master's Certificate from him and try him for manslaughter. We think that this was a measure destined to calm the opinions of the inhabitants of Halifax who, having suffered much demanded punishments which these men did not merit.

But yesterday evening we read in the dispatches displayed on the front of the newspaper *Le Harve-Eclair* that Captain Le Medec and his pilot were to be tried for manslaughter: a friend has written us from New York that he was assured that the Canadian Government was demanding from our Government, authorisation to punish very severely M. Le Medec and to imprison him.

We request you, M. le Ministre, to refuse this authorisation. You must have a thorough knowledge of this unhappy affair in all its details. You know that Captain Le Medec had no hand in the collision. He abandoned his ship presuming she was going to explode, but he could not foresee the results of his action.

You know also that if there was negligence, it consisted of bringing in, in order to join the convoy, a ship constituting a gigantic mine, in a roads confined by narrows and further restricted by the ships moored there. It is inconceivable that the captain of this vessel, who was only carrying out his orders, should be victimised. We shall be grateful to you, M. le Ministre, if you will protect him.

Trusting you will kindly take our letter into consideration, we ask you to accept, M. le Ministre, our sincere thanks and the assurance of our respectful devotion.

REGNIER,
Secretary General.

Later, the cases against Mackey and Le Medec were disposed of on habeas corpus proceedings, leaving only the charge against Commander Wyatt for the consideration of the grand jury; and on March 21, 1918, Mr. Justice Russell instructed the jury that the case against him fell short of the requirements for an indictment of manslaughter, and the charge was dropped.

Mackey, who, following the report of the inquiry, had been suspended, was later reinstated as a pilot and completely vindicated.

No action whatever was taken by the French government against Le Medec, and he went on to serve the Compagnie Générale Transatlantique until 1922. In January 1931, after he had retired from the sea, he was promoted Chevalier de la Légion d'Honneur.

Although Wyatt was cleared of the manslaughter charge against him, in deference to popular clamour in Halifax, the chief examining officer, an officer of first-rate ability and record, was transferred away from the port.

On board *Niobe,* his successor was mercilessly chaffed about his fate, if by any mischance he, too, should fall into disfavour with the Haligonians. This harmless banter served well as a cover for the wardroom's deeper feeling of disgust over the whole affair.

A royal commission was set up, in the light of the facts revealed before the wreck commissioners' inquiry, to investigate the Halifax Pilotage Commission, and its recommendations resulted in sweeping reorganization.

On January 11, 1918, when the fate of the three accused men still hung in the balance, the Lloyd's agent in Halifax cabled London as follows: "OWNERS OF MONT BLANC FILED SUIT HERE TODAY IN ADMIRALTY COURT AGAINST OWNERS OF IMO CLAIMING TWO MILLION DOLLARS DAMAGES."

The owners of the *Imo* immediately entered a counterclaim against the owners of the *Mont Blanc* for the same amount. The action was subsequently tried in the Exchequer Court before, surprisingly enough, Mr. Justice Drysdale. It was then agreed between the parties that the evidence taken before the wreck commissioners' court should, with that of one additional witness examined orally on the stand, be taken as the evidence submitted in the action. Drysdale, in his judgement, found the *Mont Blanc* solely to blame for the collision, and the Compagnie Générale Transatlantique entered an appeal in the Supreme Court of Canada.

Here, the five judges who considered the case allowed the appeal, and held that both ships were equally liable.

When, in their turn, the South Pacific Whaling Company appealed against the decision of the Supreme Court to the Lords of the Judicial Committee of the Privy Council in London, Viscount Haldane, Lord Dunedin, and Lord Atkinson were unanimous in their ruling:

> Their Lordships have thus examined critically and at great length the evidence bearing upon the points in issue in the action. They have upon the whole come to the following conclusions:
>
> First, that the *Mont Blanc,* from the time she passed the *Highflyer* till she starboarded her helm in the agony of the collision, never left her own water, though she may, no doubt, before she was actually struck, have forged ahead so as to cross the middle line of the channel.
>
> Second, that as she steamed up through her own waters her speed was not immoderate.
>
> Third, that the *Imo* in order to inflict the injury to the *Mont Blanc,* which it is proved she did inflict must have struck that ship with more force and at a higher rate of speed than her witnesses admit.
>
> Fourth, that the *Mont Blanc* must at the time of the collision have had little, if any, way on her, else the stem of the *Imo* would have been twisted to some extent, which it was not.

Fifth, that the inclination of their Lordships' opinion is that the *Imo* could, when she first reversed her engines, have crossed into and remained in her own water, as she was bound to do, but never did.

It is not necessary, however, absolutely to decide this last point, because in the case of both ships it is clear that their navigators allowed them to approach within 400 feet of each other on practically opposite courses, thus incurring the risk of collision, and indeed practically bringing about the collision, instead of reversing their engines and going astern, as our assessors advise us, they, as a matter of good seamanship, could and should have done, long before the ships came so close together. This actually led to the collision. The manoeuvre of the *Mont Blanc,* in the agony of the collision, may not have been the best manoeuvre to adopt, and yet, in the circumstances, was excusable. But their Lordships are clearly of opinion that both ships are to blame for their reciprocal neglect above-mentioned to have reversed and gone astern earlier than they did.

They are therefore of opinion that the appeal and cross-appeal both fail, that the judgement appealed from should be affirmed, and they will humbly advise His Majesty accordingly.

EPILOGUE

Estimates of the loss of life and the total casualties in the disaster varied greatly for some time, but finally the Halifax Relief Commission listed them as 1,963 killed, 9,000 injured, and 199 blinded.

Many people in the city, though, consider the Commission's figure for the number killed wildly inaccurate. F. C. MacGillivray, now chief of the Halifax fire department, who worked with the rescuers until well into the following spring, noted that during that time, he was called upon to provide more than 3,200 markers for the dead. Few believe that the Commission took into account the fatalities on board ships in the harbour or the hundreds of citizens who disappeared without a trace.

Some 25,000 people were left without adequate shelter after the explosion; 6,000 lost their homes altogether. The blast and the flames between them destroyed over 1,600 buildings, and 12,000 more were damaged. The total property loss and cost of repairs was put at $35,000,000.

For their heroic actions on December 6, 1917, posthumous awards were made of the Albert Medal in gold to Lieutenant Commander T. K. Triggs, RN, HMS *Highflyer*; and the Albert

Medal to Acting Bo'sun Albert Charles Mattison, RCN, who commanded the steam pinnace from *Niobe* and to Stoker Petty Officer Edward S. Beard, RCNVR, one of the crew of the pinnace.

The Albert Medal was also awarded to the sole survivor of the *Highflyer*'s whaler, Able Seaman William Becker, RN, and for their part in extinguishing the fire aboard the tug *Musquash,* to Leading Seaman Thomas Neil Davis, RN, and Able Seaman Robert Stones, RN.

Chief Master-at-Arms John T. Gammon, RCN, received the OBE, and Able Seaman Walter J. Critch, RNR, the Meritorious Service Medal.

The *Imo,* after lying crippled on the Dartmouth shore for more than four months, was refloated. On July 28, 1918, she arrived in New York, under tow, for repairs.

Eventually, rechristened *Guvernören,* she went to sea again as a whale oil tanker. In 1921 she was on a voyage from Norway to the Antarctic when, only twenty miles from her destination, she struck a rock. Her crew was taken off and, as salvage was impossible, on December 3, just three days before the fourth anniversary of the Halifax explosion, she was abandoned to the sea.

ACKNOWLEDGEMENTS

Icannot adequately express my gratitude to the many people who contributed so much to this book, but my especial thanks go to those whose stories I have used throughout. To Lillian Atkins, now Mrs. Boyd, living in Yarmouth, NS; to Mrs. Alex Fraser, who still has her home in Dartmouth, NS; and to Edith O'Connell, who suffered and lost so much in the disaster, now Mrs. Ralph Lowe of Dartmouth, NS.

To Rear Admiral P. W. Brock, CB, DSO, of Surrey, who graciously lent me the fascinating journal he kept at the time, which was so invaluable. To K. A. Mackenzie of London, Ontario, whose injuries later cost him the loss of an eye and forced his retirement from the Royal Canadian Navy. To Lieutenant Colonel T. S. Frowd of Dorset, who not only contributed his own experience, but sent me an illuminating account of the disaster written by his father and published in *Chambers's Journal;* and to W. D. Fowlie, now manager of the Halifax branch of the Canadian Overseas Telecommunication Corporation, whose hospitality during my stay in Nova Scotia will long be remembered, and whom I have come to look upon as a friend.

I am also deeply appreciative of the help given to me by Frank Mackey, Halifax, pilot of the *Mont Blanc;* Mrs. T. K. Triggs, who sent me a photograph of her husband and treasured mementos; G. P. Coleman, QC, Halifax, who supplied the photograph and details concerning his father, Vincent Coleman; C. J. Burchell, QC, Halifax, who gave me first-hand information concerning the inquiry and legal actions which followed the explosion; and Major and Mrs. W. C. Borrett, who greatly facilitated my research in the city.

Many hundreds of people, both in Britain and Canada, gave me their accounts and impressions of the disaster, and they are too numerous to list. I would like, however, to make special mention of the following eye-witnesses, who, through furnishing written accounts, through the loan of contemporary letters and diaries, or by patiently submitting to a searching cross-examination, provided so many essential facts and solved many of the mysteries of December 6, 1917. Although many now have their homes outside Canada, I have indicated where they were at the time of the explosion.

P. G. Bacon, SS *Borderer*
Mrs. Sydney Chapman, Halifax
Mrs. R. K. Churchill, Halifax
R. W. Cooley, Halifax
B. Crosthwaite, SS *Cairnross*
E. T. Davies, SS *Picton*
Forrester Durkee, 63rd Regiment, Halifax
W. A. Frawley, Halifax
George P. Judge, Halifax
Mrs. J. Kell, Halifax
W. C. King, SS *Iroquois*
A. Knight, HMCS *Niobe*
P. Knight, HMS *Changuinola*
J. J. Lawson, HMCS *Niobe*

Richard M. Lee, HMS *Columbella*
F. C. MacGillivray, Halifax
Mrs. R. L. McIntire, Halifax
W. McLaurin, HMCS *Hochelaga*
V. Magnus, HMS *Changuinola*
R. W. Minter, HMS *Trojan*
W. Nickerson, Halifax
Mrs. T. H. Perry, Halifax
Captain H. C. Pinsent, RN, HMCS *Niobe*
Mrs. H. C. Pinsent, Halifax
T. C. Prosser, HMS *Changuinola*
Dr. C. A. Simpson, Halifax
Cecil Stewart, Halifax
C. Sydenham, SS *Picton*
A. C. Tedder, Halifax
Bert Wetmore, Halifax
J. Forrest Whiteley, Halifax
A. H. Wickens, RCN, Halifax
T. H. Wilcock, HMS *Highflyer*
L. P. Wilkie, SS *Corfu Castle*

Official sources and public bodies have been equally co-operative, and I have to thank the admiralty for permission to quote from the reports in their docket on the disaster, and the Privy Council, and in particular L. W. S. Upton, the registrar, for making available to me the transcript of the wreck commissioners' inquiry and the decisions of the Courts of Appeal. Considerable assistance was also forthcoming from:

In Great Britain
F. A. Hawkes, Lloyd's shipping editor, and his staff; II. Watson Jamer, agent general for the Canadian Atlantic provinces in London; the British Museum Reading Room and Newspaper

Library at Colindale; the Imperial War Museum; the National Maritime Museum; the City of Westminster Reference Library; the *Daily Telegraph;* the *Times Literary Supplement; History Today; Sea Breezes;* Messrs. Harland & Wolff Limited; Messrs. Elders & Fyffes Limited; and Messrs. Evan Thomas Radcliffe & Co. Limited.

In Canada

The Canadian Broadcasting Corporation in Halifax, and in particular G. F. Brickenden, regional programme director; Miss Mary Cameron of the Halifax Memorial Library; Dr. C. Bruce Fergusson, BA, MA, D.Phil., of the Nova Scotia Archives; Frank W. Doyle, executive editor, *Halifax Herald;* Musée Maritime, Quebec; and the editors of the *Yarmouth Light* and *New Glasgow News.*

In France

Compagnie Générale Transatlantique, Paris, owners of the *Mont Blanc;* Ministère des Affaires Étrangères, Paris; Ministère d'État, Archives de France, Paris; Ministère des Armees (Marine), Paris; and *Le Figaro,* Paris.

In Norway

The shipping company A/S Thor Dahl, Sandfjord; Ole Wang, Tönsberg; Knut Berg, Oslo; and *"Krigsforsikringen,"* Oslo.

There has been little accurate or detailed material published on the disaster. The newspaper and magazine articles that are available are, in the main, sensational and unreliable, just about the only exception being the first-rate account by H. B. Jefferson in the *Atlantic Advocate.* Contemporary British and Canadian newspapers were the source of much vital information, as were the *United States Naval Institute Proceedings;* the *Official History of the Naval Service of Canada;* the American journals *Survey* and *Literary Digest;* the *British Legion Journal,* which published J. T. Gammon's own story, and the report of Major H. G. Giddings, commanding officer of the Massachusetts State Guard Halifax Relief Unit, which was kindly made available to me by his son, Robert P. Giddings.

Of inestimable value was the brilliant sociological study of the disaster *Catastrophe & Social Change,* written by Samuel Henry Prince and published by Columbia University.

I also owe a great debt for background material on the city of Halifax to Thomas H. Raddall's wonderful book *Halifax: Warden of the North,* and Hugh MacLennan's *Barometer Rising* made further worthwhile reading on the subject.

From all over the world, people sent me photographs, booklets, newspaper cuttings, letters, and other material, and special mention must be made of E. C. Young, Huntsville, Ontario, who contributed so many of the photographs that have been used throughout this book.

Finally, my heartfelt thanks go out to Wilfred Granville for his encouragement, his guidance, and his help in checking the manuscript; to Harold Hersee for his great assistance in research and his unflagging enthusiasm; and to my wife who, despite my storms and temperaments, stuck calmly to her typewriter and saw the whole thing through to its conclusion.

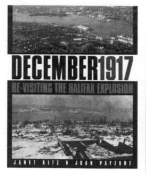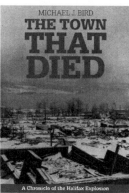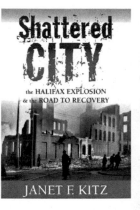